MASTERING IELTS SPEAKING PART 1

The 5W1H IELTS Speaking Blueprint

A Strategic Guide For Students and Trainers

SCORE BEYOND IELTS

MR. SINGH

ISBN 979-8-89133-944-6

CONTENTS

PREFACE

In the intricate tapestry of language learning and testing, the IELTS exam holds a prominent position as a reliable weaver of dreams for countless aspirants looking to study, work, or settle in English-speaking nations. As an experienced educator and observer of the challenges faced by these aspirants, I identified a gap – a need for a focused, structured guide, particularly for the Speaking Part 1 of the IELTS exam, which often sets the tone for the test taker's performance in the subsequent sections.

IELTS Speaking Part 1, while seemingly simple, carries the weight of first impressions. It demands not just the accuracy of language but also the precision of thought, clarity of expression, and the ability to navigate questions with finesse. With these considerations in mind, this guidebook was conceived and crafted.

This book is not merely a compilation of questions and answers. It is, more importantly, a framework, a methodology encapsulated in the 5W1H approach – Who, What, When, Where, Why, and How. Each question in the Speaking Part 1 is dissected through this lens, providing the test taker with a clear, navigable roadmap to construct answers that are not just correct but also coherent, comprehensive, and captivating.

Designed with careful attention to the nuances of the exam and the diverse profiles of the candidates, the guide offers a treasure trove of examples, scenarios, and sample answers, making it universally relevant and applicable. Whether you are a student burning the midnight oil to perfect your responses or a trainer guiding your wards through the maze of IELTS preparation, this guide is intended to be your companion, mentor, and a reliable resource.

Through the pages of this book, you'll find not just theoretical knowledge but also practical insights, tips, and strategies to approach Speaking Part 1 with confidence and calmness. It aims to demystify the process, making it less daunting and more approachable for every candidate who aspires to score high in IELTS Speaking.

In crafting this guide, my endeavor has been to simplify the complex, to clarify the obscure, and to shine a light on the path to success in IELTS Speaking Part 1. I hope that as you turn the pages, you find clarity, gain confidence, and, most importantly, move closer to realizing your dreams.

Happy reading and practicing!

Mr. Singh

Score Beyond IELTS

HOW TO USE THIS BOOK

Navigating through this comprehensive guidebook is straightforward and user-friendly, designed with the busy student and dedicated trainer in mind. Follow these steps to unlock the full potential of this resource:

1. **Understand the Framework:** Begin by familiarizing yourself with the 5W1H approach outlined in the introduction. This framework forms the backbone of the strategies and techniques discussed in the book.

2. **Start with the Basics:** Each section kicks off with foundational questions related to a specific topic. These questions are accompanied by meticulously crafted answers, serving as examples of the application of the 5W1H strategy.

3. **Practice and Reflect:** After understanding the basics, proceed to practice with the extensive set of questions provided. Reflect on the sample answers, analyzing the usage of the 5W1H approach in each.

4. **Engage with Idioms and Phrases:** Interspersed throughout the book are idioms and phrases designed to embellish your language. Practice incorporating these into your responses for a natural and fluent expression.

5. **Self-Evaluation:** Engage in self-assessment by answering the questions independently before referring to the sample answers. This practice enhances self-awareness and aids in identifying areas requiring improvement.

6. **Utilize for Teaching:** For trainers, this guide serves as an indispensable teaching aid. Direct your students to specific sections, engage in focused practice, and utilize the sample answers as benchmarks for evaluation.

For Students:

- Review the book section by section, taking time to practice and internalize the strategies discussed.

- Use the sample answers as a reference, not a script. The aim is to develop the ability to formulate your own responses using the 5W1H framework.

For Trainers:

- Assign relevant sections to students based on their learning needs and areas requiring improvement.

- Use the questions for practice sessions, and the sample answers for discussion and analysis.

Final Tips:

- Consistent practice is key. Dedicate time daily to work through the questions and formulate answers.

- Engage in peer review. Practice with a partner, providing and receiving feedback for continuous improvement.

With a structured approach to practice and a clear understanding of the 5W1H framework, success in IELTS Speaking Part 1 is not just a possibility; it's a guarantee!

ADVENTURE AND EXTREME SPORTS

1. Have you ever tried any extreme sports?

5W1H Ideas:
Who: I
What: tried an extreme sport
When: a couple of years ago
Where: near Fatehgarh Sahib
Why: for the thrill and to challenge myself
How: after taking a brief training session

Answer: A couple of years ago, near Fatehgarh Sahib, I decided to challenge myself and dived into an extreme sport after a brief training. The adrenaline rush was unlike any other. Pushing one's limits, especially in the beautiful backdrop of our town, was a truly invigorating experience.

2. Which adventure sports are popular in your region?

5W1H Ideas:
Who: Locals and tourists
What: indulge in adventure sports
When: mainly during the favorable seasons
Where: around Fatehgarh Sahib
Why: for the thrill and to enjoy the natural beauty
How: either solo or with organized groups

Answer: Around Fatehgarh Sahib, both locals and tourists eagerly partake in adventure sports, especially during the favorable seasons. The blend of natural beauty and the thrill of these activities makes it quite enticing. Whether going solo or with organized groups, there's always something adventurous on the horizon.

3. Do you think adventure sports are too risky?

5W1H Ideas:
Who: I ,
What: have an opinion about the risks
When: since I first learned about them
Where: generally speaking
Why: because of the inherent dangers associated with them
How: by comparing them with regular sports

Answer: Always having had an interest in sports, I've often weighed the pros and cons of adventure sports compared to regular ones. While there's an inherent danger in adventure sports, it's the risk that often heightens the thrill for many enthusiasts.

4. Why do you think people are attracted to extreme sports?

5W1H Ideas:
Who: People, especially youth
What: are drawn to extreme sports
When: in the modern era
Where: globally
Why: for the adrenaline rush and sense of achievement
How: by overcoming fears and physical challenges

Answer: In today's fast-paced era, many, including the youth, seek that adrenaline rush and sense of accomplishment that extreme sports offer. Overcoming fears and physical challenges gives them a unique sense of satisfaction that's hard to find elsewhere.

5. Is there an adventure sport you'd never try? Why?

5W1H Ideas:
Who: I
What: have reservations about certain adventure sports
When: after learning about them
Where: both locally and globally
Why: due to personal fears
How: by weighing the risks involved

Answer: After acquainting myself with various extreme activities, both locally and elsewhere, I've realized bungee jumping is something I'd probably steer clear of. The sheer thought of free-falling with just a cord attached is daunting to me, irrespective of the safety measures.

6. How do you prepare for an adventure sport?

5W1H Ideas:
Who: I or anyone interested
What: prepare thoroughly
When: before attempting any sport
Where: in training centers
Why: to ensure safety and to enjoy the experience fully
How: by training, learning about the sport, and using safety gear

Answer: Before plunging into any adventure sport, preparation is key. Just as many, I'd train, learn extensively about the sport, and never compromise on safety gear. This not only ensures a safer experience but also enhances the enjoyment of the sport.

7. Do you believe adventure sports should be included in school curriculums?

5W1H Ideas:
Who: Schools
What: consider including such sports
When: as part of their regular curriculum
Where: across schools
Why: for holistic development and teaching teamwork
How: by organizing trips and training sessions

Answer: I'm of the belief that schools should contemplate integrating adventure sports into their curricula. Beyond the thrill, they foster teamwork, resilience, and holistic development, equipping students with skills that transcend the classroom.

8. Are children encouraged to take up adventure sports in your area?

5W1H Ideas:
Who: Children and young adults
What: sometimes take up such sports
When: during vacations or weekends
Where: in and around Fatehgarh Sahib
Why: for physical activity, building confidence, and learning new skills
How: under the guidance of trained professionals

Answer: In and around Fatehgarh Sahib, children, especially during school breaks or weekends, are occasionally introduced to adventure sports. Under the watchful eyes of trained professionals, these activities not only offer physical exertion but also instill confidence and impart valuable life skills.

ANIMALS AND PETS

1. Do you have any pets?

5W1H Ideas:
Who: I
What: have a pet
When: since a few years ago
Where: at my home
Why: for companionship and the joy they bring
How: by adopting from a local shelter

Answer: Yes, for the past few years, I've had a pet dog at my home. I adopted him from a local shelter because I sought companionship, and the bond we share is truly heartwarming.

2. What's your favorite animal?

5W1H Ideas:
Who: I
What: have a favorite animal
When: always, since childhood
Where: among all the animals I've encountered
Why: because of its unique characteristics and appeal
How: after reading and observing them

Answer: Since my childhood, among the many animals I've come across, I've always been enamored with dolphins. This affection grew as I observed their unique behavior and read about their captivating characteristics.

3. Are there any animals you're afraid of?

5W1H Ideas:
Who: I
What: have a fear of certain animals
When: since a specific incident in childhood
Where: especially when I encounter them unexpectedly
Why: due to a past experience or their appearance
How: by either facing or avoiding them

Answer: Since a peculiar incident in my childhood, I've held an apprehensive feeling towards snakes. Whenever I encounter them, especially unexpectedly, my instinct is to avoid them, a response perhaps rooted in that past experience or their daunting appearance.

4. Have you ever been to a zoo or wildlife sanctuary?

5W1H Ideas:
Who: I
What: visited a zoo or wildlife sanctuary
When: a couple of years ago
Where: in my city
Why: to observe animals and learn about them
How: on a day trip with friends/family

Answer: A couple of years back, I ventured to a wildlife sanctuary in Chandigarh. It was during a day trip with friends, and the primary motivation was to observe animals in their habitats and understand their behaviors more intimately.

5. Do you think pets benefit our health?

5W1H Ideas:
Who: Many people, including me
What: experience health benefits
When: while spending time with them
Where: at home
Why: pets provide companionship, reduce stress,
How: by interacting, playing with them

Answer: I'm among the many who firmly believe in the health benefits pets bring. At home or even in therapeutic settings, their companionship reduces stress and boosts physical activity. It's through daily interactions and moments shared with them that we truly feel these positive effects.

6. What is the most common pet in your area?

5W1H Ideas:
Who: People in my area
What: common pet
When: currently and in recent years
Where: in my locality
Why: possibly due to the pet's adaptability or popularity
How: by observing or interacting with neighbors and friends

Answer: In my locality, over recent years, it's been evident that cats are the most common companions people have. Their adaptability to our environment or perhaps their innate charm might be reasons for this trend. It's something I've noticed during interactions with neighbors and friends.

7. Do you believe wild animals should be kept as pets?

5W1H Ideas:
Who: I
What: have a stance on keeping wild animals as pets
When: given the ongoing debates and after observing instances
Where: globally and especially in regions with exotic pet trades
Why: due to ethical, safety concerns
How: after reading, discussing, and witnessing the challenges wild pets face

Answer: Given the ongoing discussions and what I've observed, I believe wild animals shouldn't be kept as pets. My stance stems from various reasons, from ethical concerns to safety issues. Especially in regions with a rampant exotic pet trade, the challenges these animals face make it clear that their place isn't within domestic settings.

8. Have you ever watched a documentary on animals?

5W1H Ideas:
Who: I
What: watched a documentary
When: a few months ago
Where: at home on a streaming platform
Why: to understand and appreciate wildlife better
How: during a weekend relaxation session

Answer: Yes, a few months ago, I delved into an animal documentary while relaxing at home. It was on a streaming platform, and my primary motivation was to gain a deeper understanding and appreciation for wildlife. Such visuals always leave me in awe of the natural world.

ARCHITECTURE AND BUILDINGS

1. Do you have a favorite style of architecture?

5W1H Ideas:
Who: I
What: have a favorite architectural style
When: after exploring various designs and structures over the years
Where: both locally and during travels
Why: due to its aesthetic appeal and historical significance
How: by observing and appreciating various architectural wonders

Answer: Over the years, after witnessing various architectural marvels both locally and during my travels, I've developed a penchant for Gothic architecture. Its aesthetic allure combined with its historical gravitas is what draws me to it.

2. Are there any famous buildings or landmarks in your hometown?

5W1H Ideas:
Who: Residents of my hometown, I
What: recognize and value them
When: since their establishment
Where: in my hometown
Why: they represent cultural or historical significance
How: by visiting, learning about, or just admiring them

Answer: Absolutely, my hometown boasts of The Clock Tower, which holds both cultural and historical relevance. It's been a point of recognition for ages, and most of us residents take immense pride in it.

3. What kind of buildings do you find most appealing?

5W1H Ideas:
Who: I
What: have a preference for designs
When: after exploring diverse buildings
Where: in various cities and towns
Why: due to their uniqueness
How: by evoking feelings of admiration and awe in me

Answer: Throughout my travels and explorations of various cities, I've always been drawn to Art Deco or Colonial buildings. Their unique designs, rich histories, or sheer functionalities never cease to instill admiration and awe in me.

4. How do you feel about skyscrapers dominating city skylines?

5W1H Ideas:
Who: Urban dwellers, including me
What: observe the rise of skyscrapers
When: over the past few decades
Where: in metropolitan areas globally
Why: they symbolize development but also raise concerns
How: by changing the skyline and influencing urban development.

Answer: Watching skyscrapers dominate city skylines, especially over the past few decades, is awe-inspiring but also brings mixed feelings. They stand as symbols of progress and development, yet I can't help but think of the congestion and environmental concerns they sometimes represent.

5. What do you think of modern architecture compared to older styles?

5W1H Ideas:
Who: I
What: have an opinion on this
When: after seeing the evolution
Where: in cities, museums, and sites
Why: based on preferences and functionality
How: by comparing

Answer: Having witnessed the architectural transition over time, in various cities and historical sites, I feel modern designs prioritize functionality and sustainability. While older styles have undeniable aesthetic charm, contemporary architecture seems to better address today's urban challenges.

6. Would you prefer living in traditional house or a modern apartment?

5W1H Ideas:
Who: I
What: have a living preference
When: considering my current lifestyle and needs
Where: when thinking about settling or relocating
Why: based on comfort, convenience,
How: by weighing the pros and cons

Answer: Given my current lifestyle and requirements, I'd lean towards both. While traditional houses exude a rustic charm, modern apartments often offer convenience and a sense of community. It's always a balance between the two for me.

7. Do you believe that buildings can influence our mood or behavior?

5W1H Ideas:
Who: I and many psychologists
What: believe in the psychological impact of architectural designs
When: after experiences and studies
Where: in various indoor and outdoor environments
Why: it can influence lighting, space perception, and overall ambiance
How: by evoking emotions and impacting our daily actions

Answer: Undoubtedly, based on personal experiences and numerous studies, I'm convinced that architectural designs profoundly influence our moods and behaviors. The way lighting, space, and ambiance are curated in a building can evoke a myriad of emotions and affect our daily actions.

8. Are there any historical buildings in your area?

5W1H Ideas:
Who: Local residents and tourists
What: visit and admire these buildings
When: all year round, especially during cultural events
Where: in my area
Why: they hold historical significance and cultural value
How: by preserving them

Answer: Absolutely, in my area, there's an old fort which stands as a testament to our rich history. Locals and tourists alike flock to it, especially during cultural events, to soak in its architectural brilliance and historical tales.

ART AND CREATIVITY

1. Do you enjoy visiting art galleries or museums?

5W1H Ideas:
Who: I
What: visit art galleries and museums
When: during weekends or holidays
Where: in various cities I've been to
Why: to appreciate art and understand cultural history
How: by observing, reading about, and sometimes participating in interactive exhibits.

Answer: Absolutely, I often find myself wandering through art galleries and museums during weekends or holidays. They offer a rich tapestry of art and cultural history, and each visit is a journey of discovery and appreciation.

2. How do you feel about modern art compared to classical art?

5W1H Ideas:
Who: Art enthusiasts, including me
What: have opinions on these
When: after viewing various artworks
Where: in galleries, exhibitions
Why: based on personal aesthetic preferences and the emotions evoked
How: by analyzing techniques, themes, and the messages conveyed

Answer: Modern art and classical art evoke different feelings in me. While I appreciate the technique and timelessness of classical pieces, modern art's abstract nature and bold messages intrigue and challenge me.

3. Have you ever tried creating your own artwork?

5W1H Ideas:
Who: I
What: attempted to create artwork
When: in my free time or in art classes
Where: at home or in an art studio
Why: to express myself or just experiment with creativity
How: using paint, clay, or digital tools

Answer: Yes, I've dabbled in creating my own artwork, both at home and during art classes. Whether it was experimenting with paint, molding clay, or even digital art, it's always been a journey of self-expression and creative exploration.

4. Who's your favorite artist, and why?

5W1H Ideas:
Who: I **What:** have a favorite artist
When: after exploring various artworks
Where: in galleries, online platforms
Why: due to their unique style, themes, or the emotions their work evokes in me
How: by deeply connecting with the artist's work and philosophy

Answer: Over the years, after immersing myself in various art forms, I've been particularly drawn to Leonardo Da Vinci. There's something about his unique style and the deep emotions his artwork conveys that resonates with me profoundly.

5. What forms of art are most popular in your country?

5W1H Ideas:
Who: Residents and tourists
What: appreciate and celebrate art
When: at various festivals and events
Where: especially in cultural hubs
Why: because they represent the nation's culture, history, and heritage
How: through exhibitions, performances, and workshops

Answer: In my country, forms like traditional dance or pottery hold immense popularity. They are not just art forms; they represent our rich culture and history. At various festivals and events, you'll find these arts being celebrated with great enthusiasm.

6. Do you prefer hand-made art or digital art?

5W1H Ideas:
Who: I
What: have a preference between these
When: after experiencing both forms
Where: in art exhibitions and online
Why: based on the feel, texture, and connection I sense with the artwork
How: by assessing the techniques, authenticity, and personal resonance

Answer: While I greatly admire the precision and possibilities of digital art, there's an authenticity and tactile feel to hand-made art that I deeply cherish. The personal touch and the imperfections make it more relatable and genuine to me.

7. Do you think art classes should be mandatory in schools?

5W1H Ideas:
Who: Educators, parents, and policymakers
What: consider the importance of art
When: during curriculum planning and academic discussions
Where: in schools and institutes
Why: to foster creativity, cultural appreciation, and holistic development
How: by integrating regular art lessons and activities into the school program

Answer: I firmly believe that art classes play a pivotal role in fostering creativity and ensuring a well-rounded education. Making them mandatory would not only boost cultural appreciation but also cater to the holistic development of students.

8. Do you think children should be encouraged to take up art classes?

5W1H Ideas:
Who: Parents, educators
What: encourage children to engage
When: during their formative years
Where: in schools or private art centers
Why: to foster creativity, self-expression, and cognitive development
How: by providing the resources, guidance, and a conducive environment

Answer: Absolutely, children in their formative years stand to gain immensely from art classes. It's not just about fostering creativity, but also aiding their cognitive development and self-expression. The colors, shapes, and techniques offer them a unique language to explore.

BOOKS AND READING

1. How often do you read books?

5W1H Ideas:
Who: I
What: read books
When: almost daily, especially before bed
Where: at home, in parks, or travelling
Why: for relaxation, knowledge, and entertainment
How: by setting aside dedicated time and immersing myself in the story

Answer: Reading is my daily sanctuary. Be it at home, a park, or even during commutes, I often find solace in the pages of a book. It's a perfect blend of relaxation, knowledge acquisition, and sheer entertainment.

2. What genre of books do you prefer?

5W1H Ideas:
Who: I
What: have a preferred genre
When: after reading over the years
Where: in bookstores, libraries,
Why: as they resonate with my interests and emotions
How: by deeply connecting with the themes and narratives of that genre

Answer: Over time, I've gravitated towards historical fiction. The rich tapestry of past events blended with imaginative storytelling captivates me, offering both knowledge and a riveting narrative.

3. How do you feel about e-books compared to traditional paper books?

5W1H Ideas:
Who: I
What: have feelings about them
When: after using both formats
Where: at home, traveling, or when free
Why: based on tactile experience, convenience, and natural concerns
How: by assessing the reading experience, portability, and impact.

Answer: While e-books offer undeniable convenience and portability, there's a tangible connection I feel with traditional paper books. The rustling of pages, the book's weight, and even its smell brings a sensory richness that's hard to replicate digitally.

4. How do you choose what books to read?

5W1H Ideas:
Who: I
What: select books
When: whenever looking for a new read
Where: in bookstores, online reviews, or based on recommendations
Why: to ensure I enjoy and benefit
How: by researching, getting insights from others, and my mood or interests

Answer: When on the hunt for a new book, I usually rely on a mix of online reviews, personal recommendations, and my current mood. Browsing through bookstores and gauging the first few pages also influences my choice, ensuring I dive into a worthwhile read.

5. What was the last book you read and how did you find it?

5W1H Ideas:
Who: I
What: read Rich Dad Poor Dad
When: recently
Where: at home during my leisure time
Why: based on its reputation and intriguing synopsis
How: by dedicating a few hours each day until completion

Answer: I recently delved into Rich Dad Poor Dad, which I picked up due to its rave reviews. Engrossing myself in its pages at home, I found the narrative captivating, providing both entertainment and thought-provoking insights.

6. Are there any authors from your country that you would recommend?

5W1H Ideas:
Who: I
What: recommend local authors
When: asked about literature from my region
Where: to anyone interested
Why: to showcase the richness of our literary heritage
How: by suggesting notable works

Answer: Absolutely! Our literary landscape is rich with talent. I'd highly recommend Amrita Pritam who beautifully captures the essence and nuances of our culture through her writings.

7. Do you think reading habits have changed due to technology?

5W1H Ideas:
Who: Modern readers and technology users
What: undergo shifts in reading habits
When: with the rise of e-readers, audiobooks, and digital platforms
Where: globally, across all age groups
Why: for convenience, accessibility
How: by adopting new tech platforms and adjusting reading patterns

Answer: Certainly, with the digital age upon us, reading habits have undergone a transformation. While traditional books hold their charm, the convenience and vast library offered by e-readers and audiobooks have certainly reshaped the reading landscape.

8. Do you believe schools should focus more on encouraging reading for pleasure?

5W1H Ideas:
Who: Educators, parents, and policymakers
What: emphasize reading for enjoyment
When: in academic year and holidays
Where: in schools and at home
Why: to foster a love for reading, improve comprehension, and expand horizons
How: by creating diverse libraries and promoting book clubs

Answer: Absolutely! Schools, while ensuring academic rigor, should also cultivate a love for reading. Encouraging reading for pleasure can enhance comprehension, expand horizons, and instill a lifelong passion for literature.

CHILDHOOD MEMORIES

1. What's your earliest childhood memory?

5W1H Ideas:
Who: I, as a young child
What: experienced playing in the rain
When: at the age of four or five
Where: in the courtyard of my ancestral home in Punjab
Why: because it was a moment of pure joy and discovery
How: embracing the raindrops, laughing and playing with siblings

Answer: One of my earliest memories is of playing in the rain outside our ancestral home in Punjab. I was around four or five, and I recall the sheer elation, the sound of laughter mingling with raindrops as I frolicked with my siblings.

2. Did you have a favorite toy as a child?

5W1H Ideas:
Who: I
What: had a wooden horse
When: throughout my early childhood
Where: at home, and occasionally it accompanied me on outings
Why: because it was a gift
How: taking care of it, playing imaginative games, and keeping it close

Answer: Oh, I fondly remember my wooden horse toy, a constant companion throughout my early years. Gifted by a dear uncle, its sentimental value made it more than just a plaything. Whether at home or on outings, it was always by my side.

3. Were there any childhood games you loved playing?

5W1H Ideas:
Who: I, along with friends and siblings
What: played hide and seek
When: during long summer evenings or after school
Where: in the fields or alleys near home
Why: for fun, camaraderie
How: with excitement, inventing new rules, and sharing laughter

Answer: The simple joys of childhood! I fondly remember playing hide and seek with friends and siblings. Those long summer evenings or post-school hours, wandering the fields or local alleys, were filled with laughter, camaraderie, and the thrill of the game.

4. How did you celebrate your birthdays as a child?

5W1H Ideas:
Who: I, my family, and friends
What: celebrated birthdays
When: annually
Where: at home, with decorations, cake,
Why: to acknowledge the joy of life and milestones
How: by throwing a small party, cutting a cake, and sharing moments

Answer: Birthday celebrations were homely affairs. With the house adorned in decorations, the aroma of delicious food, and the anticipation of cake and gifts, I'd eagerly await the company of friends and family. It was always about love, laughter, and cherished memories.

5. Is there any childhood tradition you particularly remember?

5W1H Ideas:
Who: My family and I
What: lighting lamps
When: during Diwali
Where: at our home in Punjab
Why: to honor our cultural heritage and pass down family customs
How: with devotion, joy, and familial bonding

Answer: A childhood tradition close to my heart is lighting lamps during Diwali. Our home in Punjab would come alive with shimmering lights, resonating with joy and devotion. It wasn't just about the festival, but the warmth and bond of our family coming together.

6. Did you have a childhood friend who was very close to you?

5W1H Ideas:
Who: I and Aman
What: shared a deep bond of friendship
When: from early primary school years
Where: in school, at each other's homes
Why: common interests, and our personalities meshed well
How: by sharing secrets, playing games, and supporting each other

Answer: Aman was my childhood confidante. From our school days and neighborhood games to shared secrets under starry skies, our bond was unbreakable. Our mutual interests and complementary personalities made us inseparable.

7. Were there any places you loved visiting as a child?

5W1H Ideas:
Who: I, with my family
What: visited the local fair
When: during holidays
Where: a few kilometers away from our home
Why: it was a source of joy, excitement, and family bonding
How: enjoying the rides, savoring the food, and experiencing the atmosphere

Answer: The local fair was a childhood favorite. A short journey from our home, it was a world of wonder during holidays. The exciting rides, the tantalizing aroma of street food, and the family bonding it offered are memories I cherish.

8. What kind of stories did you enjoy hearing as a child?

5W1H Ideas:
Who: My grandparents or parents
What: narrated folktales
When: during bedtime
Where: in the cozy corners of our home
Why: to entertain, impart values, and cultivate a love for stories
How: with animated voices, vivid descriptions, and sometimes, even little enactments

Answer: Bedtimes were magical with the folktales my grandparents spun. Nestled in the comfort of our home, their animated voices and vivid imaginations transported me to enchanted realms. These tales weren't just stories but life lessons wrapped in allure.

CHILDHOOD TOYS AND GAMES

1. Which toy was your favorite when you were a child?

5W1H Ideas:
Who: I
What: cherished my toy train
When: during my early childhood years
Where: at home
Why: it was a gift from my grandparents and sparked my imagination
How: by playing with it, imagining different scenarios, and sometimes sharing it with friends

Answer: My toy train was the star of my childhood. Gifted by my loving grandparents, it occupied a special place in my room. It was more than just a toy; it was the key to countless imaginative journeys.

2. Did you play any traditional games growing up?

5W1H Ideas:
Who: I, along with my friends
What: played games like kabaddi
When: during evenings and weekends
Where: in our backyard or the park
Why: they were fun, helped in bonding, and were part of our cultural heritage
How: forming teams, setting rules, and competing in friendly matches

Answer: Kabaddi and marbles were the essence of my evenings. In the community park, with friends and cousins, we'd dive into these traditional games. They weren't just about winning; they were our cultural legacy and bond.

3. Did you have a soft toy or teddy bear that you were attached to?

5W1H Ideas:
Who: I
What: had a fluffy bunny
When: from my toddler years to early teens
Where: it was mostly by my bedside
Why: it was a comforting presence and a gift from my mother
How: by cuddling it during sleep

Answer: A fluffy bunny was my childhood comforter. A gift from my mother, it sat faithfully by my bedside. It wasn't just a toy; it was a symbol of warmth and security.

4. Were board games a part of your childhood activities?

5W1H Ideas:
Who: I, with my family
What: played Monopoly and Chess
When: on weekends
Where: in the living room
Why: they were entertaining, intellectually stimulating,
How: by setting up the board, understanding rules, and engaging

Answer: Monopoly and Chess were the stars of our family nights. Gathered in the living room, we'd immerse ourselves in these board games. Beyond the fun, they strengthened our bonds and sharpened our minds.

5. How often did you play outside with other kids?

5W1H Ideas:
Who: I and the neighborhood kids
What: played various outdoor games
When: almost every evening
Where: in the nearby park
Why: to enjoy the fresh air, socialize, and engage in physical activity
How: by organizing different games, forming teams,

Answer: Almost every evening, the streets of our locality or the nearby park echoed with our laughter. Teaming up with neighborhood kids, we dived into myriad outdoor games. It was more than play; it was our daily dose of camaraderie and vitality.

6. Do you think toys and games from your childhood are different from today's?

5W1H Ideas:
Who: I, comparing then and now
What: notice differences between past and present toys and games
When: while reflecting upon my past and observing kids today
Where: at homes, stores, playgrounds
Why: due to technological changes
How: by seeing more digital games, advanced toys,

Answer: When I cast my mind back and juxtapose my childhood games with today's, the contrast is evident. While we reveled in traditional toys and outdoor escapades, today's young ones are engrossed in high-tech gadgets and virtual playgrounds.

7. Were puzzles or building blocks a part of your playtime?

5W1H Ideas:
Who: I
What: played with them
When: during rainy days or indoor playtime
Where: in my room or the living area
Why: they were intellectually stimulating and enhanced creativity
How: by challenging myself to complete puzzles or construct intricate structures

Answer: Certainly, Puzzles and building blocks were my rainy-day companions. On days when playing outside wasn't feasible, I'd engross myself in these creative endeavors, pushing my limits and constructing imaginative wonders.

8. Did you ever exchange or trade toys with friends?

5W1H Ideas:
Who: I and my friends
What: occasionally exchanged or traded toys
When: during school breaks
Where: at school or each other's homes
Why: to experience something new without buying
How: by discussing our interests, setting terms, and sometimes even bartering

Answer: Exchanging toys was a ritual of sorts among my friends and me. Be it during playdates or school breaks, we'd often barter favorites, each seeking a fresh play experience without the need for a new purchase.

DANCING AND PERFORMANCE ARTS

1. Have you ever taken dancing lessons?

5W1H Ideas:
Who: I
What: attended dancing lessons
When: during my teenage years
Where: at a local dance academy
Why: to learn the art of dancing and express myself creatively
How: by enrolling in a six-month beginner's course

Answer: During my teenage years, I enrolled in a local dance academy for a six-month beginner's course. Dancing intrigued me as it offered a unique medium to express myself creatively.

2. What's your favorite dance style or performance art?

5W1H Ideas:
Who: I
What: have a preference for a specific dance style
When: ever since I witnessed it live
Where: at a cultural event in my city
Why: because of its grace, rhythm, and cultural significance
How: by watching various dance styles and being captivated by this one

Answer: Ever since I witnessed a mesmerizing live performance at a cultural event in my city, I've been smitten by bhangra. Its grace, rhythm, and cultural depth simply resonates with me.

3. Are there famous dance or performance art events in your country?

5W1H Ideas:
Who: Local and international audience
What: attend prominent events
When: annually or during festivals
Where: across various cities
Why: to experience, celebrate, and promote the rich artistic heritage
How: through grand showcases, competitions, and exhibitions

Answer: Absolutely! There are several iconic dance and art events held across the country, drawing both local and international attendees. Held annually or during particular cultural festivals, such as bhangra, garbha, these events are a testament to our rich artistic tapestry.

4. Would you consider attending a dance or performance art show?

5W1H Ideas:
Who: I
What: contemplate attending a dance or art performance
When: in the near future
Where: in a renowned theater
Why: to appreciate the art form and enjoy a cultural experience
How: by inviting a friend family member

Answer: Absolutely! Given the chance, I'd love to attend a dance or art performance in a renowned theater or cultural hub. Sharing such a cultural experience with a friend or family, in the near future, sounds truly enriching.

5. How do you feel when you watch a live dance performance?

5W1H Ideas:
Who: I
What: feel a range of emotions
When: during a live dance performance
Where: in a theater, an auditorium
Why: due to the dancers' expressions, movements, and the music
How: by being immersed and letting the performance evoke emotions in me

Answer: Whenever I watch a live dance performance, it's a roller coaster of emotions for me. The dancers' expressions, coupled with the rhythm and music, immerse me fully, making me feel connected to each moment.

6. Did your school offer dance as a subject or extracurricular activity?

5W1H Ideas:
Who: My school
What: provided dance classes
When: throughout my schooling years
Where: within the school's auditorium
Why: to promote the arts and offer a creative outlet for students
How: by hiring professional dance instructors and organizing annual performances

Answer: Yes, during my school years, dance was offered both as a subject and an extracurricular activity. With skilled instructors at the helm and an annual showcase, it was a wonderful way for students to embrace the arts.

7. Are there any traditional dances specific to your region or country?

5W1H Ideas:
Who: People of my region or country
What: perform and cherish such dances
When: during festivals, celebrations
Where: in community gatherings, festivals, and cultural events
Why: to celebrate heritage, history
How: by teaching younger generations, organizing dance events, and ensuring its preservation

Answer: Certainly! In my region, there are distinctive traditional dances such as bhangra and giddha celebrated during various festivals and events. These dances are more than just movements; they echo our heritage, narrate our history, and bind the community together.

8. Do you think modern dance forms will replace traditional ones in the future?

5W1H Ideas:
Who: The younger generation
What: may lean towards modern dance
When: in the foreseeable future
Where: worldwide, especially in urban areas
Why: due to globalization, evolving preferences, and media influence
How: by popularizing contemporary styles through media, workshops, and competitions

Answer: While the allure of modern dance forms is undeniably strong, especially with media influence, I believe traditional dances have an enduring charm. Though preferences evolve, the depth and heritage of traditional dances will always find a place in the heart of culture.

DAILY ROUTINES

1. When do you usually wake up in the morning?

5W1H Ideas:
Who: I
What: wake up
When: every morning
Where: in my bedroom
Why: to start my day and fulfill my responsibilities
How: naturally or with the help of an alarm

Answer: Every morning, like clockwork, I find myself waking up at 5 in the serene environment of my bedroom. To ensure I'm up and about for my daily tasks, I often rely on my trusty alarm clock.

2. What's the first thing you do after waking up?

5W1H Ideas:
Who: I
What: engage in a morning routine
When: right after waking up
Where: in my bedroom or bathroom
Why: to freshen up and start the day right
How: by stretching, brushing my teeth, and washing my face

Answer: The moment I rise and shine, I indulge in a brief stretch to awaken my senses. Following that, it's off to the bathroom to brush my teeth and splash my face with water, ensuring I'm all set for the day ahead.

3. How do you usually commute to work or school?

5W1H Ideas:
Who: I
What: commute
When: on weekdays or whenever required
Where: to my workplace or school
Why: to attend classes or fulfill my job responsibilities
How: either by bus, car, bike, or on foot

Answer: On typical weekdays, my journey to work is quite systematic. Depending on the weather and my mood, I might opt for the bus, take a refreshing bike ride, or even enjoy a leisurely walk.

4. What tasks do you prioritize during the first half of your day?

5W1H Ideas:
Who: I
What: handle important tasks
When: in the first half of my day
Where: at my workplace or home office
Why: to ensure they get my freshest energy and attention
How: by making a to-do list or setting reminders

Answer: The morning hours for me are crucial. At my workplace, I dive into the most pressing tasks, ensuring they get my undivided attention. A handy to-do list or a set reminder often guides me in this process.

5. How do you prefer to spend your evenings after a long day?

5W1H Ideas:
Who: I
What: relax and unwind
When: during the evenings
Where: at home or occasionally out with friends
Why: to rejuvenate and take a break
How: by reading, watching a movie, or engaging in a hobby

Answer: After a bustling day, evenings are my sanctuary. At home, you'll often find me engrossed in a captivating book or perhaps watching a movie. Occasionally, a night out with friends adds a perfect touch to the day.

6. Do you follow a specific routine before going to bed?

5W1H Ideas:
Who: I
What: adhere to a bedtime routine
When: every night
Where: in my bedroom and bathroom
Why: to relax and ensure a good night's sleep
How: by reading, meditating, or performing skincare rituals

Answer: Each night, I cherish a set routine to wind down. My bedroom turns into a tranquil sanctuary where I might delve into a few pages of a book, meditate, or indulge in some skincare. These rituals pave the way for restful sleep.

7. How often do you change or adjust your daily routine?

5W1H Ideas:
Who: I
What: modify my daily routine
When: occasionally or as circumstances demand
Where: in my day-to-day life
Why: to adapt to new tasks or commitments
How: by reassessing my priorities and making tweaks

Answer: Life's unpredictable nature means I occasionally need to adjust my daily routine. Whether it's a new commitment or a shifting priority, I'm always ready to reassess and make the necessary tweaks to keep things flowing smoothly.

8. Do you have any weekend routines that differ from weekdays?

5W1H Ideas:
Who: I
What: have distinct weekend routines
When: on Saturdays and Sundays
Where: at home or other recreational spots
Why: to relax, recharge, and indulge in personal interests
How: by pursuing hobbies, spending time with family, or visiting new places

Answer: Weekends usher in a change of pace for me. While weekdays are all about work and tasks, Saturdays and Sundays are my canvas, painted with hobbies, quality time with family, and exploring new places around town.

DREAMS AND ASPIRATIONS

1. What is your biggest dream in life?

5W1H Ideas:
Who: I
What: have a major aspiration
When: in the foreseeable future
Where: in my professional and personal life
Why: to achieve personal satisfaction and make a difference
How: by working hard, staying committed, and continually learning

Answer: My most significant dream is to meld my personal and professional life in a way that not only grants me satisfaction but also leaves a lasting impact. With dedication, perseverance, and an insatiable thirst for learning, I believe I can turn this vision into reality.

2. Have your dreams changed over time?

5W1H Ideas:
Who: I
What: witnessed an evolution in my dreams
When: as I grew older and experienced more of life
Where: in various stages of my life
Why: due to changing circumstances, knowledge, and priorities
How: naturally and influenced by life's lessons

Answer: As the chapters of my life have unfolded, so have the contours of my dreams. Growth, experiences, and life's myriad lessons have painted them in different hues, reflecting the ever-evolving journey of self-discovery.

3. How do you plan to achieve your aspirations?

5W1H Ideas:
Who: I
What: have a strategy
When: for the upcoming years
Where: in my career and personal development
Why: to make my dreams a tangible reality
How: through careful planning, continuous effort, and seeking guidance

Answer: Turning dreams into reality requires more than just wishful thinking. I've charted out a roadmap for the coming years, filled with milestones, and action points. With consistent effort, unwavering commitment, and seeking wisdom from those who've walked the path before, I'm determined to see my aspirations come to fruition.

4. Who or what inspires your dreams?

5W1H Ideas:
Who: Various individuals and experiences
What: Inspire and shape my aspirations
When: Throughout my life
Where: In different scenarios, both personal and professional
Why: To give direction and motivation
How: By setting examples, imparting wisdom, or challenging me

Answer: Throughout my journey, I've been blessed to encounter individuals such as my father who've etched indelible marks on my aspirations. Be it through their actions, wisdom, or the challenges they've thrown my way, they've continually steered me toward my goals.

5. Do you discuss your dreams with others or keep them private?

5W1H Ideas:
Who: I
What: Sometimes share my dreams
When: When I seek advice or feel the need to vocalize them
Where: With close friends, family, or mentors
Why: To get feedback, motivation, or simply to speak them into existence
How: Candidly, with trust and hope

Answer: While many of my dreams remain personal, I occasionally share them with close friends, family, or mentors. Speaking them aloud, especially to those who understand and support me, adds another layer of reality and sometimes provides invaluable feedback.

6. Do you think it's better to have big dreams or more realistic ones?

5W1H Ideas:
Who: I
What: Value both types of dreams
When: Throughout different phases of life
Where: Depending on the situation and what I aim to achieve
Why: Because both serve different purposes and are equally essential
How: By balancing optimism with practicality

Answer: In the tapestry of dreams, I find value in weaving both grand visions and realistic aspirations. While big dreams offer boundless motivation and a broader perspective, realistic goals ensure tangible progress and steady momentum.

7. Have you ever given up on a dream? Why?

5W1H Ideas:
Who: I
What: Have reconsidered certain aspirations
When: As I evolved and my priorities changed
Where: In the journey of life
Why: Due to changing circumstances, self-growth, or better opportunities
How: By reflecting, seeking counsel, and understanding myself better

Answer: Yes, there have been instances where dreams once held dear were left behind. As I traversed the maze of life, growth and newfound insights often reshaped my desires. Some dreams were replaced by more profound aspirations, while others simply paved the way for better opportunities.

EDUCATION AND LEARNING

1. What was your favorite subject in school and why?

5W1H Ideas:
Who: I
What: Loved history
When: During my school years
Where: In the classroom and during independent studies
Why: It provided insights into past civilizations and cultural evolutions
How: Through engaging narratives and detailed study

Answer: During my school years, history held a special place in my heart. Delving into the tales of past civilizations and understanding cultural shifts was always riveting. It was like piecing together a grand puzzle of human evolution.

2. Do you believe in lifelong learning? Why or why not?

5W1H Ideas:
Who: I
What: Strongly believe in the concept of lifelong learning
When: Throughout life's journey
Where: In both professional and personal spheres
Why: Continuous learning helps in personal growth and adapting to changing times
How: By seeking knowledge, being curious, and embracing change

Answer: Absolutely! I'm a staunch advocate for lifelong learning. It's essential not just for personal evolution but also for adapting to our ever-evolving world. By constantly feeding our curiosity and embracing change, we stay relevant and enriched.

3. How do you prefer to study: alone or in groups?

5W1H Ideas:
Who: I
What: Prefer studying alone
When: Especially during crucial study sessions
Where: In a quiet and focused environment
Why: It allows for deep concentration and understanding
How: By creating a dedicated study space and minimizing distractions

Answer: I've always leaned towards solitary study sessions. In a tranquil environment, free from distractions, I feel my concentration deepens, allowing me to grasp concepts more effectively.

4. Did you enjoy school when you were younger?

5W1H Ideas:
Who: I
What: Had a good time in school
When: During my younger years
Where: At my local school
Why: I had supportive teachers and great friends
How: By participating in various activities and focusing on studies

Answer: Absolutely, my younger years in school were filled with fond memories. Thanks to supportive teachers and a circle of fantastic friends, every day was an enriching experience.

5. Which teacher do you remember the most? Why?

5W1H Ideas:
Who: I
What: Recall my English teacher vividly
When: Throughout my high school years
Where: In the school's English department
Why: She was inspiring and genuinely cared about our learning
How: By going beyond the curriculum and introducing us to classic literature

Answer: My high school English teacher stands out in my memories. Her passion for the subject and commitment to our learning journey was unmatched. She went the extra mile, introducing us to classic literature and igniting a love for reading.

6. How did you travel to school every day?

5W1H Ideas:
Who: I
What: Used to take the bus
When: Every school day
Where: From home to school
Why: It was convenient and economical
How: By catching the school bus at the nearby stop

Answer: I used to catch the school bus every day. With a bus stop conveniently located nearby, it was not only economical but also a fun way to start and end the school day.

7. Do you still keep in touch with your school friends?

5W1H Ideas:
Who: I
What: Maintain contact with a few close school friends
When: Even now, years after graduation
Where: Through social media and occasional meetups
Why: We share a strong bond and cherish those memories
How: By prioritizing our friendship and keeping the communication lines open

Answer: Yes, even after all these years, I remain in touch with a handful of my school friends. The bond we formed back then still holds strong. Thanks to social media and occasional meet-ups, we manage to keep our connection alive.

8. Did you join any clubs or groups in school?

5W1H Ideas:
Who: I
What: Was a part of the debate club
When: Throughout high school
Where: In the school's club activities
Why: I had a penchant for public speaking and critical thinking
How: By actively participating in club meetings and representing the school in competitions

Answer: During high school, I was an active member of the debate club. My love for public speaking and critical thinking drew me to it. Not only did I participate in our internal sessions, but I also had the honor of representing our school in various competitions.

FAMILY AND FRIENDS

1. How many people are there in your family?

5W1H Ideas:
Who: My family members
What: Consists of five people
When: Currently
Where: Living together in our home
Why: It's my immediate family
How: My parents, two siblings, and I make up the family

Answer: Currently, there are five of us in my family. It's my parents, my two siblings, and myself. We all live together in our cozy home.

2. Who are you closest to in your family?

5W1H Ideas:
Who: I
What: Share a close bond
When: Since childhood
Where: Within the family
Why: We understand and support each other
How: Through shared experiences and mutual understanding

Answer: I've always had a special bond with my younger sibling since our childhood. We've been through thick and thin together and share a deep understanding.

3. Do you often meet up with your friends?

5W1H Ideas:
Who: I and my friends
What: Meet regularly
When: Almost every weekend
Where: At cafes, parks, or someone's house
Why: To catch up and spend quality time
How: By coordinating our schedules and planning activities

Answer: Yes, my friends and I make it a point to meet up almost every weekend. We usually hang out at cafes, parks, or sometimes at one of our houses, cherishing our moments together.

4. What qualities do you value in a friend?

5W1H Ideas:
Who: I
What: Value certain qualities
When: While forming and maintaining friendships
Where: In personal relationships
Why: To ensure trust and understanding
How: By observing their behavior and interactions over time

Answer: When it comes to friendships, I deeply value honesty, loyalty, and understanding. It's essential for me to trust my friends and feel a genuine connection with them.

5. Do you prefer spending time with family or friends?

5W1H Ideas:
Who: I
What: Enjoy spending time
When: During free hours or weekends
Where: Home or outside
Why: Each offers a unique experience and comfort
How: By dividing my time between family gatherings and friend meetups

Answer: That's a tough one. While I cherish the comfort and bond of family gatherings, I also relish the laughter and adventures with my friends. So, it's a balance for me.

6. Do you have any siblings?

5W1H Ideas:
Who: My siblings
What: Are my family members
When: Since birth
Where: In our family home
Why: We are born to the same parents
How: Naturally, as part of the family structure

Answer: Yes, I have two siblings, and we've grown up together in our family home, sharing countless memories.

7. How often do you see your grandparents?

5W1H Ideas:
Who: My grandparents
What: Meet
When: Usually on weekends or special occasions
Where: At their house or ours
Why: To spend quality time and bond
How: By visiting them or inviting them over

Answer: I usually see my grandparents on weekends or special occasions. We often visit each other's homes to spend quality time.

8. What do you usually do with your friends?

5W1H Ideas:
Who: My friends and I
What: Hang out
When: On weekends or after work/school
Where: At local spots or someone's house
Why: To relax and catch up
How: Organizing meetups or impromptu plans

Answer: My friends and I typically hang out at local spots or at someone's house on weekends or after work, just to relax and catch up.

9. Who is the oldest member of your family?

5W1H Ideas:
Who: My great-grandmother
What: Is the oldest
When: Currently
Where: Within our extended family
Why: She's lived the longest
How: By virtue of age

Answer: The oldest member of our family is my great-grandmother. She's a treasure trove of stories and experiences.

10. Do you have any cousins?

5W1H Ideas:
Who: My cousins
What: Are relatives
When: Since birth
Where: Part of the extended family
Why: We share common grandparents
How: Through familial ties

Answer: Yes, I have several cousins. We share a close bond and often meet during family gatherings

FASHION AND CLOTHING

1. What kind of clothes do you usually wear?

5W1H Ideas:
Who: I
What: Wear casual and comfortable clothes
When: On a regular basis
Where: For everyday activities
Why: I prioritize comfort and practicality
How: By choosing relaxed fit clothes, soft fabrics, etc.

Answer: On a regular basis, I lean towards casual and comfortable clothes. Whether I'm running errands or simply lounging, I always prioritize comfort.

2. Do you have a favorite color to wear?

5W1H Ideas:
Who: I
What: Prefer certain colors
When: When choosing clothes
Where: In my wardrobe selection
Why: I feel they complement my personality
How: By often gravitating towards those shades

Answer: Yes, I've always been partial to blues. Somehow, I feel the color complements my personality and mood quite well.

3. How often do you shop for clothes?

5W1H Ideas:
Who: I
What: Shop
When: Occasionally, mostly during sales or season changes
Where: At local stores or online
Why: To update my wardrobe or replace worn-out items
How: By browsing and purchasing what catches my eye

Answer: I shop for clothes occasionally, especially during sales or when the seasons change. It's a mix of updating my wardrobe and replacing items that have seen better days.

4. Do you wear traditional clothes?

5W1H Ideas:
Who: I
What: Sometimes wear traditional attire
When: On festivals or special family occasions
Where: At family gatherings or cultural events
Why: To honor my culture and traditions
How: By dressing up in ethnic wear

Answer: Yes, I do wear traditional clothes, especially during festivals or special family occasions. It's a wonderful way to honor and connect with my culture.

5. Are you fond of accessories?

5W1H Ideas:
Who: I
What: Like wearing accessories
When: Depending on the occasion and outfit
Where: With my regular attire
Why: They accentuate and complete my look
How: By matching or contrasting them with my outfits

Answer: Absolutely! I believe accessories play a pivotal role in accentuating an outfit. Depending on the occasion, I love adding a necklace or a pair of earrings to complete my look.

6. Do you have a favorite item of clothing?

5W1H Ideas:
Who: I
What: Have a cherished clothing item
When: Since I bought it last year
Where: From a boutique downtown
Why: It fits perfectly and boosts my confidence
How: By pairing it with different accessories and outfits

Answer: Yes, I have this shirt I bought from a boutique downtown last year. It fits like a dream and instantly boosts my confidence every time I wear it.

7. How do you decide what to wear every day?

5W1H Ideas:
Who: I
What: Choose my clothes
When: Every morning
Where: In my bedroom
Why: Depending on my mood, the weather, and my plans for the day
How: By checking the weather forecast, my schedule, and listening to how I feel

Answer: Every morning, in my bedroom, I decide what to wear based on the weather, my plans, and honestly, my mood. It's a blend of practicality and intuition.

8. Do you follow fashion trends?

5W1H Ideas:
Who: I
What: Occasionally follow trends
When: When a new season begins
Where: Through fashion magazines and online platforms
Why: To update myself and sometimes add new pieces to my wardrobe
How: By observing what's popular and trying out what appeals to me

Answer: I occasionally follow fashion trends, especially when a new season rolls around. I like to keep updated, picking up cues from magazines and online platforms, and if something resonates with me, I might add it to my wardrobe.

9. Do you prefer comfort or style?

5W1H Ideas:
Who: I
What: Prioritize comfort but like style
When: Always, when choosing clothes
Where: In my everyday clothing choices
Why: Comfort is paramount but I also like to look presentable
How: By finding a balance between comfortable fabrics and trendy designs

Answer: While I always prioritize comfort, I do have an inclination for style. I believe in finding that sweet spot where comfortable meets chic.

10. How has your style evolved over the years?

5W1H Ideas:
Who: I
What: Have seen changes in my fashion choices
When: Over the years
Where: From school days to now
Why: Due to changing preferences, trends, and maturity
How: Gradually, influenced by experiences and exposure

Answer: Over the years, my style has certainly evolved. From my school days to now, changing trends, personal preferences, and maturity have all played their part. It's been a gradual journey, shaped by my experiences and exposure.

FESTIVALS AND CELEBRATIONS

1. Which festival do you enjoy the most?

5W1H Ideas:
Who: I
What: Enjoy Diwali the most
When: Annually, usually in October or November
Where: At home with family
Why: Because of the lights, sweets, and the spirit of togetherness
How: By decorating our home, lighting lamps, and exchanging gifts

Answer: I absolutely cherish celebrating Diwali. It's an annual festival, around October or November, where our home is filled with lights, delicious sweets, and the warmth of family. The spirit of togetherness during this festival makes it very special for me.

2. How do you usually celebrate your birthday?

5W1H Ideas:
Who: I
What: Celebrate my birthday
When: Once a year, on my birth date
Where: Varies, but usually at home or a restaurant
Why: To mark the passage of another year and enjoy with loved ones
How: By cutting a cake, spending time with family and friends, and sometimes throwing a party

Answer: I usually celebrate my birthday either at home or a cozy restaurant. It's a day filled with cake cutting, time spent with close ones, and sometimes a little party. It's all about marking another year and making memories.

3. Do you think festivals are losing their traditional touch?

5W1H Ideas:
Who: I
What: Feel that some festivals are becoming more commercialized
When: In recent years
Where: In many parts of the world
Why: Due to commercialization and globalization
How: By being more about shopping and gifts and less about traditions

Answer: In recent years, I've observed that some festivals, in various places, are veering towards commercialization. The essence of tradition sometimes gets overshadowed by shopping and gifting, which is a bit disheartening.

4. How important are festivals in your culture?

5W1H Ideas:
Who: For us, the people in my culture
What: Consider festivals as significant events
When: Throughout the year
Where: In our region and among our communities
Why: They signify traditions, values, and moments of togetherness
How: By dedicating specific days to celebrate, uphold traditions, and gather together

Answer: Festivals hold a prominent place in our culture. Throughout the year, we have various celebrations that signify our traditions, values, and the bond we share as a community. They are moments that weave us together, cherishing our roots.

5. Are there any international festivals or celebrations you admire?

5W1H Ideas:
Who: I
What: Admire Christmas
When: Every December
Where: Celebrated worldwide
Why: Because of its universal message of peace, joy, and giving
How: By observing the decorations, music, and the spirit of the festival

Answer: I've always been fond of Christmas, celebrated every December across the globe. The universal themes of peace, joy, and the act of giving that it promotes resonate with me deeply. It's heartwarming to see the festive decorations and hear the joyous music.

6. Do you enjoy traditional dances and music during festivals?

5W1H Ideas:
Who: I
What: Enjoy traditional dances and music
When: During festivals
Where: At festivals in our locality or on TV
Why: They bring out the cultural essence and are vibrant
How: By watching performances and sometimes even participating

Answer: Absolutely, during festivals, I love indulging in the sights and sounds of traditional dances and music. Whether it's live in our locality or on TV, the vibrancy and cultural essence it brings is truly captivating.

7. Is there a local festival you think everyone should experience once?

5W1H Ideas:
Who: Tourists or outsiders
What: Experience a local festival, say Lohri
When: Annually
Where: In our region, particularly Punjab
Why: It provides a unique cultural immersion
How: By joining the locals in their celebrations

Answer: Definitely, I believe everyone should experience 'Lohri' at least once. Celebrated annually in Punjab, it offers a unique cultural immersion. Joining the locals in their celebrations would give anyone a taste of our rich traditions.

8. How do children in your family feel about festivals?

5W1H Ideas:
Who: Children in my family
What: Feel excited and joyous about festivals
When: Every time a festival approaches
Where: In our home and community
Why: They get to wear new clothes, eat sweets, and participate in fun activities
How: By eagerly participating and awaiting each festivity

Answer: The children in our family brim with excitement every time a festival approaches. With the prospect of new clothes, sweets, and the myriad of fun activities, their enthusiasm and anticipation is palpable in our home.

9. Do you have any special attire you wear during festivals?

5W1H Ideas:
Who: I
What: Wear special traditional attire
When: During festivals
Where: At home or when attending festive gatherings
Why: To honor the tradition and be a part of the festive spirit
How: By donning outfits like the kurta or salwar-kameez with traditional jewelry

Answer: Indeed, during festivals, I love to don our special traditional attire. Whether it's a 'kurta' or 'salwar-kameez', paired with traditional jewelry, it not only honors the tradition but also immerses me completely in the festive spirit.

10. Are there any festivals you wish to witness in other countries?

5W1H Ideas:
Who: I
What: Wish to witness festivals like the Rio Carnival or Chinese New Year
When: In the future
Where: In countries like Brazil or China
Why: They seem colorful, lively, and offer a different cultural perspective
How: By traveling to these countries during their festive times

Answer: Yes, I've always been intrigued by festivals like the 'Rio Carnival' in Brazil or the 'Chinese New Year'. They seem so colorful and lively. Experiencing them would offer a fresh cultural perspective, and I hope to travel to these countries during their festive times in the future.

FESTIVE FOODS

1. What's your favorite food to eat during festivals?

5W1H Ideas:
Who: I
What: Have a favorite festive food, perhaps Jalebis
When: During festivals
Where: At home or festive gatherings
Why: They are sweet, delicious, and evoke nostalgic memories
How: Freshly made by local vendors or sometimes prepared at home

Answer: During festivals, I absolutely relish eating 'Jalebis'. Whether savored at home or festive gatherings, their sweet taste and the nostalgia they bring make them my top festive treat.

2. Do you prepare any special dishes at home for festivals?

5W1H Ideas:
Who: My family and I
What: Prepare special dishes, like Samosas and Gulab Jamuns
When: On festive occasions
Where: At our home
Why: To celebrate and uphold our culinary traditions
How: Using traditional recipes handed down through generations

Answer: Certainly, every festive occasion sees my family and I preparing traditional dishes like 'Samosas' and 'Gulab Jamuns' at home. It's our way of celebrating and preserving our rich culinary traditions.

3. Are there any festive foods you haven't tried but wish to?

5W1H Ideas:
Who: I
What: Want to try different festive foods, maybe Mooncakes during the Mid-Autumn Festival
When: In the near future
Where: Maybe in a Chinese community or China itself
Why: Curiosity and love for trying new foods
How: By attending a Mid-Autumn festival celebration

Answer: I've always been curious about 'Mooncakes' that are savored during the Mid-Autumn Festival. My love for exploring new foods has me eager to try them, hopefully by attending a celebration in a Chinese community someday.

4. Do festivals influence your diet a lot?

5W1H Ideas:
Who: I
What: Adjust my diet
When: During the festival season
Where: At home and festive gatherings
Why: Due to the abundance of special foods and treats
How: By indulging a bit more than usual and sometimes overeating

Answer: Indeed, festivals do have a knack for influencing my diet. With the abundance of delightful foods and treats during the season, I tend to indulge a tad more, sometimes even overeating.

5. Are there any foods you only eat during certain festivals?

5W1H Ideas:
Who: I and many in our community
What: Eat specific foods, like   Makki di Roti and Sarson da Saag during Lohri
When: Specifically during certain festivals like Lohri
Where: At home or community gatherings
Why: They hold cultural significance and are traditional
How: Prepared freshly and enjoyed with family and friends

Answer: Absolutely, there are foods like 'Makki di Roti and Sarson da Saag' that I particularly savor during Lohri. These dishes hold a special cultural significance and are best enjoyed during this festival with family and friends.

6. Is there a festive food that reminds you of your childhood?

5W1H Ideas:
Who: I
What: Recall festive foods from childhood, such as   Besan ke Laddoo
When: Back when I was a child
Where: At my grandparents' house
Why: Because it was a treat my grandmother made every festival
How: By following a special recipe she learned from her mother

Answer: Certainly, every time I taste 'Besan ke Laddoo', it transports me to my childhood. It was a treat my grandmother prepared every festival at her house, using a special recipe handed down from her mother.

7. Do you enjoy cooking festive foods yourself?

5W1H Ideas:
Who: I
What: Enjoy cooking festive dishes, perhaps Peda and Kaju Katli
When: Especially during festive seasons
Where: In my kitchen
Why: I love the process and the joy it brings
How: By following traditional recipes and sometimes giving them a modern twist

Answer: Absolutely, I thoroughly enjoy whipping up festive dishes, especially 'Peda' and 'Kaju Katli'. It's a delightful process, and I often follow traditional recipes, occasionally adding my own modern twist.

8. Do you prefer sweet or savory festive foods?

5W1H Ideas:
Who: I
What: Have a preference between sweet and savory
When: Whenever I indulge in festive foods
Where: At festive gatherings or at home
Why: Based on my taste buds' liking
How: I usually lean more towards one type based on my mood

Answer: It's a tough call, but I would say I lean slightly more towards sweet festive foods. There's something about the richness and flavor that resonates with celebrations for me.

9. Are there any festive foods you don't like?

5W1H Ideas:
Who: I
What: Not particularly fond of some festive foods, maybe Mathi
When: Whenever it's served during festivals
Where: At different festive occasions
Why: Maybe it's the taste or texture that doesn't sit well with me
How: I've tried it several times, but it's just not to my liking

Answer: Well, while I appreciate the wide array of festive foods, I've never quite taken a liking to 'Mathi'. I've tried it on multiple occasions, but something about its taste or texture just doesn't resonate with me.

10. Do you think festive foods are becoming more modernized nowadays?

5W1H Ideas:
Who: People in general
What: Modernizing festive foods, like Chocolate Diyas for Diwali
When: In recent years
Where: Across many cultures and communities
Why: To innovate and keep up with changing tastes
How: By infusing traditional foods with modern flavors or presentations

Answer: Certainly, there's a noticeable trend where traditional festive foods are getting a modern makeover. For instance, the emergence of 'Chocolate Diyas' for Diwali is a testament to how people are blending tradition with contemporary tastes.

FOOD AND COOKING

1. What's your favorite meal to prepare at home?

5W1H Ideas:
Who: I
What: Have a favorite meal, perhaps Butter Chicken with Naan
When: Usually on weekends or special occasions
Where: In my kitchen at home
Why: Because it's delicious and reminds me of family gatherings
How: Using my mother's special recipe

Answer: I absolutely cherish preparing 'Butter Chicken with Naan' at home. It's typically a weekend treat, and I follow my mother's special recipe. The rich flavors remind me of family gatherings.

2. Do you prefer eating out or cooking at home?

5W1H Ideas:
Who: I
What: Have a preference between eating out and home-cooked meals
When: On most days
Where: Either at a restaurant or my own kitchen
Why: Based on convenience, taste, or mood
How: Sometimes by mood, other times by schedule

Answer: While I enjoy the occasional restaurant outing, I mostly lean towards home-cooked meals. There's a certain warmth and authenticity to them that's hard to replicate.

3. How often do you try new recipes?

5W1H Ideas:
Who: I
What: Experiment with new recipes
When: Occasionally, maybe once a month
Where: In my kitchen
Why: To expand my culinary skills and try new flavors
How: By exploring recipe books or online tutorials

Answer: Once in a blue moon, about every month, I dive into a new recipe. Whether it's from a cookbook or an online tutorial, I love expanding my culinary horizons.

4. Are there any traditional dishes from your region that you love to cook?

5W1H Ideas:
Who: I
What: Enjoy cooking traditional dishes, perhaps Sarson da Saag with Makki di Roti
When: Especially during winters
Where: At my home
Why: Because it's a regional favorite and very nutritious
How: Using fresh mustard greens and corn flour

Answer: Absolutely, come winter and I'm often seen preparing 'Sarson da Saag with Makki di Roti'. It's not just a regional favorite but also packed with nutrition.

5. What do you think is the hardest dish you've ever prepared?

5W1H Ideas:
Who: I
What: Prepared a challenging dish, maybe Biryani
When: A while back for a special occasion
Where: In my kitchen
Why: Wanted to test my culinary skills
How: With meticulous attention to detail and lots of patience

Answer: I'd say crafting a perfect 'Biryani' was a culinary challenge for me. The layers, spices, and the precise cooking time required meticulous attention and patience.

6. Is there any food you dislike?

5W1H Ideas:
Who: I
What: Dislike certain foods, maybe brussels sprouts
When: Since childhood or after a particular experience
Where: First tried at home or a particular restaurant
Why: Because of the taste, texture, or a past experience
How: Avoid it or give it another chance occasionally

Answer: Yes, I've never been a fan of brussels sprouts. Since childhood, I've found their taste a bit too strong for my liking.

7. How important is a balanced diet to you?

5W1H Ideas:
Who: I
What: Value a balanced diet
When: Daily or most of the time
Where: At home, work, or even when dining out
Why: For health, energy, and overall well-being
How: By including various food groups in my meals

Answer: A balanced diet holds immense importance to me. Whether I'm at home or dining out, I always aim to incorporate various food groups for health and vitality.

8. Who taught you to cook?

5W1H Ideas:
Who: My mother, grandmother, or a cooking class
What: Taught me cooking skills
When: During my teenage years or earlier
Where: At home or in a cooking class
Why: To be self-sufficient or as a bonding activity
How: Through hands-on experience or step-by-step guidance

Answer: My mother was my culinary guru. During my early teenage years, we'd spend countless hours in the kitchen, where she'd share her secret recipes and techniques.

9. Are there any cooking shows or chefs you admire?

5W1H Ideas:
Who: I
What: Admire certain cooking shows or chefs, maybe Master Chef or Gordon Ramsay
When: During my free time
Where: On television or online streaming platforms
Why: They provide culinary inspiration and tips
How: By watching episodes or following their recipes

Answer: Definitely! I'm a big fan of 'Master Chef' and have always admired the culinary prowess of Gordon Ramsay. Their shows are a delightful blend of art and technique.

10. Do you enjoy spicy food?

5W1H Ideas:
Who: I
What: Have a preference for spicy food
When: Whenever I crave something flavorful
Where: At home or when dining out
Why: It tingles my taste buds and offers a burst of flavors
How: By adding extra chilies or spices to my meals

Answer: Absolutely! Spicy food has a special place in my heart. It just adds that extra zing and makes every meal an adventure.

FUTURE PLANS

1. Do you have any plans for the upcoming weekend?

5W1H Ideas:
Who: I
What: Plans to visit a nearby park
When: This weekend
Where: A park in the town center
Why: To relax and enjoy nature
How: Walk or cycle there with friends

Answer: Yes, I'm planning to visit a park in the town center this weekend. It's a great spot to relax and I'm looking forward to cycling there with some friends.

2. Are you thinking about any vacations for next year?

5W1H Ideas:
Who: I
What: Planning a beach vacation
When: Next summer
Where: Goa or any tropical destination
Why: To relax and enjoy the sea
How: By saving and planning the itinerary in advance

Answer: Indeed, I'm considering a beach vacation for next summer. Goa is on the top of my list. It's the perfect place to rejuvenate by the sea.

3. Have you set any personal goals for the next five years?

5W1H Ideas:
Who: I
What: Aiming for a promotion at work
When: Within the next five years
Where: At my current workplace
Why: For career growth and personal development
How: By enhancing my skills and networking

Answer: Absolutely, I aspire to climb the corporate ladder at my current workplace in the next five years. I believe enhancing my skills and expanding my network will pave the way.

4. Do you plan on learning something new soon?

5W1H Ideas:
Who: I
What: Plan to learn the Spanish language
When: Starting next month
Where: At a local language school
Why: Enhance communication skills and travel
How: By joining classes and practicing regularly

Answer: Yes, I'm keen on learning Spanish starting next month. I think it'll be beneficial for both my travels and broadening my communication skills.

5. Are there any big events you're looking forward to in the near future?

5W1H Ideas:
Who: I
What: Excited about my cousin's wedding
When: Later this year
Where: In a countryside resort
Why: To celebrate and meet extended family
How: By helping in preparations and attending ceremonies

Answer: Certainly! Later this year, my cousin's wedding is taking place at a countryside resort. It's an event I eagerly await, not just for the celebrations but also to reunite with my extended family.

6. Do you foresee any changes in your daily routine soon?

5W1H Ideas:
Who: I
What: Plan to include morning exercises
When: Starting next week
Where: At the local park or my home
Why: To improve health and start the day energetically
How: By setting an alarm and following a specific workout regimen

Answer: Yes, starting next week, I intend to incorporate morning exercises into my daily routine. Whether it's at the local park or at home, it's all about kickstarting my day with a boost of energy.

7. Are you planning to move to a new place in the future?

5W1H Ideas:
Who: I
What: Considering relocating to a new city
When: Possibly in the next two years
Where: A city with better job opportunities
Why: For career growth and a change in environment
How: By researching potential cities and preparing for the move

Answer: I'm pondering the idea of relocating to a new city, possibly in the next couple of years. A place with more job prospects would be ideal, offering both career growth and a refreshing change of environment.

8. Have you thought about pursuing further studies?

5W1H Ideas:
Who: I
What: Thinking about a master's degree
When: Maybe next year
Where: At a reputable university abroad
Why: To enhance my knowledge and open up more job avenues
How: By researching courses and applying for scholarships

Answer: Certainly, I've been contemplating pursuing a master's degree, possibly next year. I believe studying at a recognized university abroad would not only deepen my knowledge but also broaden my career opportunities.

9. Do you have any plans to take up a new hobby?

5W1H Ideas:
Who: I
What: Interested in learning pottery
When: Later this year
Where: At a nearby pottery workshop
Why: To explore a creative outlet and relax
How: By enrolling in a beginner's course

Answer: Absolutely, I've been eyeing pottery and hope to take it up later this year. I've discovered a nearby workshop that offers beginner courses, and I believe it'll be a therapeutic and creative experience.

10. Are you thinking of changing your job in the foreseeable future?

5W1H Ideas:
Who: I
What: Contemplating a career shift
When: In the coming year or so
Where: Within the same industry but a different role
Why: To challenge myself and grow professionally
How: By networking and seeking out new opportunities

Answer: In the foreseeable future, particularly in the coming year, I've been considering a career change. While I'd stay in the same industry, a different role could present new challenges and growth opportunities.

GARDENING AND PLANTS

1. Do you have a garden at your home?

5W1H Ideas:
Who: I
What: Have a small garden
When: It's been there since we moved in
Where: At the back of my house
Why: To grow fresh vegetables and enjoy the greenery
How: With the help of family, maintaining it regularly

Answer: Yes, I've had a quaint garden at the back of my house since we moved in. It's a collective effort with my family, where we grow fresh veggies and bask in its green ambiance.

2. Which plants do you like growing?

5W1H Ideas:
Who: I
What: Prefer flowering plants and herbs
When: Especially during spring and summer
Where: In the pots and beds of my garden
Why: They brighten up the space and are useful in cooking
How: By planting seeds or young plants and caring for them

Answer: I'm particularly fond of growing flowering plants and herbs. They not only embellish my garden during spring and summer but also serve as great additions to my culinary experiments.

3. Do you think gardening is a beneficial hobby?

5W1H Ideas:
Who: Many people
What: Find gardening therapeutic
When: During their free time or weekends
Where: In gardens, balconies, or terraces
Why: It's relaxing and provides a sense of achievement
How: By nurturing plants and seeing them grow

Answer: Absolutely, many find gardening to be incredibly therapeutic. Dedicating time to nurture plants, either in gardens or balconies, often brings relaxation and a profound sense of accomplishment.

4. How often do you water your plants?

5W1H Ideas:
Who: I
What: Water my plants
When: Every morning
Where: In my garden
Why: To keep them healthy and vibrant
How: Using a watering can or hose, ensuring not to overwater

Answer: Every morning, without fail, I ensure to water my plants in the garden. It's a ritual that keeps them thriving, and I use a watering can or hose, always cautious not to overdo it.

5. Do you prefer indoor or outdoor plants?

5W1H Ideas:
Who: I
What: Have a slight preference for outdoor plants
When: All year round
Where: In the garden outside
Why: They often grow bigger and are easier for me to maintain
How: By providing them ample sunlight and space

Answer: I lean slightly towards outdoor plants. They typically grow more robust under the ample sunlight in my garden, and I find them relatively easier to maintain.

6. Are there any particular flowers you love seeing in gardens?

5W1H Ideas:
Who: I
What: Love roses and lilies
When: Especially when they're in full bloom
Where: In gardens or parks
Why: They have a captivating fragrance and appearance
How: They blossom beautifully under the right conditions

Answer: Roses and lilies always captivate my attention in gardens or parks. Their alluring fragrance and stunning appearance, especially when in full bloom, are simply mesmerizing.

7. Did you ever plant a tree?

5W1H Ideas:
Who: I
What: Planted a few trees
When: On various occasions, like World Environment Day
Where: In our local park and backyard
Why: To contribute to the environment and shade
How: By digging a hole, placing the sapling, and nurturing it

Answer: Yes, I've taken the initiative to plant trees on several occasions, like World Environment Day. Whether in our local park or my backyard, it's my way of giving back to the environment.

8. Do you enjoy the company of plants inside your home?

5W1H Ideas:
Who: I
What: Keep a few indoor plants
When: Over the past few years
Where: In my living room and bedroom
Why: They purify the air and enhance aesthetics
How: By choosing specific indoor varieties and placing them in pots

Answer: Absolutely! Over the past few years, I've adorned my living room and bedroom with specific indoor plants. Not only do they uplift the ambiance, but they also purify the air.

9. Have you ever received plants as a gift?

5W1H Ideas:
Who: I, from a friend
What: Received a beautiful fern plant
When: Last birthday
Where: At my home
Why: As a symbol of growth and greenery
How: It came in a lovely pot with care instructions

Answer: Indeed, on my last birthday, a close friend gifted me a beautiful fern plant. It was a heartwarming gesture, symbolizing growth, and it even came with its care manual!

10. Do you use any apps or books for gardening tips?

5W1H Ideas:
Who: I
What: Occasionally refer to a gardening app
When: Whenever I need specific advice
Where: On my smartphone
Why: To get the best care tips and techniques
How: By browsing through the app's database and forums

Answer: Yes, when I need specialized advice, I turn to a gardening app on my smartphone. It offers a plethora of care tips and techniques, making my gardening journey a tad easier.

HEALTH AND FITNESS

1. Do you follow any fitness routine?

5W1H Ideas:
Who: I
What: Follow a fitness routine
When: Every morning
Where: At the local gym or my home
Why: To stay active and maintain good health
How: By doing a mix of cardio and strength exercises

Answer: Every morning, I commit to a fitness routine, either at the local gym or within the confines of my home. I engage in a mix of cardio and strength exercises to ensure I remain spry and sustain my well-being.

2. Do you prefer home-cooked meals or fast food?

5W1H Ideas:
Who: I
What: Prefer home-cooked meals
When: Most of the time
Where: At my home
Why: They are healthier and I can control the ingredients
How: By preparing dishes using fresh produce and minimal oil

Answer: Most of the time, I gravitate towards home-cooked meals. I relish the control over ingredients and the assurance of consuming something wholesome. Plus, the use of fresh produce and minimal oil makes it a healthier choice.

3. How often do you visit a doctor for a check-up?

5W1H Ideas:
Who: I
What: Visit the doctor
When: Once a year
Where: At the nearby clinic
Why: To ensure I'm in good health and detect any potential issues early
How: By scheduling an annual comprehensive check-up

Answer: I make it a point to see the doctor once a year at the nearby clinic. An annual comprehensive check-up reassures me of my health status and helps catch any potential health concerns early on.

4. Are you part of any sports or fitness clubs?

5W1H Ideas:
Who: I
What: Member of a local badminton club
When: Joined two years ago
Where: At a community center nearby
Why: To engage in physical activity and socialize
How: By attending weekly sessions and participating in matches

Answer: Yes, two years ago, I became a member of a local badminton club stationed at our community center. It's a fantastic blend of indulging in physical exercise and bonding with fellow enthusiasts during weekly sessions.

5. Do you believe mental health is as important as physical health?

5W1H Ideas:
Who: I
What: Strongly believe in the importance of mental health
When: Always
Where: In all aspects of life
Why: Because the mind and body are interconnected and both need attention
How: By practicing mindfulness, seeking professional help if needed, and ensuring work-life balance

Answer: I've always been an advocate for mental health, considering it paramount alongside physical health. Recognizing that the mind and body are intertwined, I practice mindfulness and prioritize work-life balance to maintain equilibrium.

6. How do you relax after a long day?

5W1H Ideas:
Who: I
What: Relax
When: After a long day
Where: In my bedroom or living room
Why: To recharge and reduce stress
How: By listening to soothing music, reading a book, or taking a short nap

Answer: After a tiring day, I usually wind down in my bedroom or living room, either immersing myself in a good book or listening to calming tunes. These activities act as a reset button, alleviating my stress.

7. Do you take any dietary supplements?

5W1H Ideas:
Who: I
What: Take dietary supplements
When: Daily
Where: At home with my meals
Why: To ensure I get all necessary nutrients
How: In the form of multivitamins and fish oil capsules

Answer: Indeed, I incorporate dietary supplements into my daily regimen. Taking them alongside my meals, I rely on multivitamins and fish oil capsules to ensure a balanced nutrient intake.

8. How much water do you drink in a day?

5W1H Ideas:
Who: I
What: Drink water
When: Throughout the day
Where: At home, work, and wherever I go
Why: To stay hydrated and maintain bodily functions
How: By carrying a reusable water bottle and refilling it several times

Answer: Throughout the day, irrespective of where I am - be it home or work - I ensure I stay hydrated. My trusty reusable water bottle, which I refill multiple times, aids in this endeavor.

9. Have you ever tried any form of alternative medicine?

5W1H Ideas:
Who: I
What: Tried acupuncture
When: Last year
Where: At a wellness center
Why: To address persistent back pain
How: Through a recommendation from a friend

Answer: Yes, last year, I ventured into alternative medicine by trying acupuncture. Aimed at alleviating my persistent back pain, I sought this treatment at a wellness center, all thanks to a friend's recommendation.

10. Do you believe in taking regular breaks while working?

5W1H Ideas:
Who: I
What: Believe in taking breaks
When: During work hours
Where: At my workplace or study area
Why: To rest my eyes, stretch my legs, and refresh my mind
How: By setting alarms or reminders every hour

Answer: Absolutely! While engrossed in work or study, I've always prioritized regular breaks. Whether it's to rest my eyes, take a brisk walk, or simply stretch, I typically set hourly alarms as reminders.

HISTORY AND CULTURAL HERITAGE

1. Do you enjoy learning about history?

5W1H Ideas:
Who: I
What: Enjoy learning about history
When: Whenever I get an opportunity
Where: In school, museums, or through books
Why: Because it provides insights into our past and how societies evolved
How: By reading, attending lectures, or watching documentaries

Answer: Absolutely! Whenever I get a chance, I dive into history, be it through books, documentaries, or museum visits. It fascinates me to understand our past and see how societies have evolved over time.

2. Is there a historical place in your town or city?

5W1H Ideas:
Who: Residents of my city
What: Visit a historical place
When: On weekends or holidays
Where: In my city
Why: To connect with our heritage and learn
How: By organizing guided tours or school trips

Answer: Yes, in my city, we have a historical monument that many locals and tourists visit, especially on weekends. It serves as a beautiful reminder of our rich cultural heritage and often hosts guided tours.

3. Do you think students should study history in school?

5W1H Ideas:
Who: Students
What: Study history
When: During their school years
Where: In school
Why: To understand past events and their influence on today's world
How: Through textbooks, lectures, and field trips

Answer: Certainly! I firmly believe that during their school years, students should delve into history. It not only acquaints them with past events but also sheds light on how past influences shape our present.

4. Have you ever attended a cultural festival?

5W1H Ideas:
Who: I
What: Attended a cultural festival
When: Last summer
Where: In the city center
Why: To immerse myself in the traditions and celebrations
How: With family and friends

Answer: Indeed, last summer, I had the joy of attending a cultural festival in our city center. Accompanied by family and friends, it was a delightful dive into traditional festivities and customs.

5. How important is it to preserve historical sites?

5W1H Ideas:
Who: Society at large
What: Preserve historical sites
When: Continuously
Where: In cities and towns
Why: To keep the memory of our ancestors alive and educate future generations
How: Through government initiatives, community efforts, and tourism

Answer: Preserving historical sites is paramount for society. Not only do they act as bridges to our past, connecting us to our ancestors, but they also serve as educational hubs for future generations. Community efforts, coupled with governmental initiatives, play a crucial role in this preservation.

6. Do you have a favorite era in history?

5W1H Ideas:
Who: I
What: Have a favorite era
When: While studying history
Where: At school or during personal reading
Why: Because of the events or the culture during that time
How: By reading about it or watching documentaries

Answer: Indeed, during my history lessons at school, I became particularly fond of the Renaissance era. The blend of art, culture, and scientific awakening during that period truly captivates me.

7. How often do you visit museums or historical sites?

5W1H Ideas:
Who: I
What: Visit museums or historical sites
When: Few times a year
Where: In various cities or during travels
Why: To gain knowledge and appreciate art and history
How: Either alone, with family, or on guided tours

Answer: A couple of times a year, I make it a point to visit museums or historical sites, whether in my city or while traveling. It's a fantastic way to soak in art, history, and culture.

8. Are there any historical movies or shows you enjoy watching?

5W1H Ideas:
Who: I
What: Enjoy watching historical movies or shows
When: During weekends or free time
Where: At home or in a cinema
Why: Because they are both entertaining and educational
How: Streaming online or watching on television

Answer: Absolutely! During weekends, I often indulge in historical movies or shows at home. They're not just entertaining; they offer a wonderful peek into past events and cultures.

9. Do you own any antiques or historical artifacts?

5W1H Ideas:
Who: I
What: Own antiques or historical artifacts
When: Acquired over the years
Where: At my home
Why: As a connection to the past or as decorative items
How: Purchased or inherited

Answer: Yes, over the years, I've collected a few antiques which adorn my home. Some were purchased, while others have been passed down through generations. They serve as beautiful remnants of the past.

10. How do you feel about restoring old buildings instead of building new ones?

5W1H Ideas:
Who: Society and architects
What: Restore old buildings
When: When considering urban development
Where: In cities or towns with historical structures
Why: To maintain cultural heritage and reduce waste
How: Through careful restoration and preservation techniques

Answer: I'm all for restoring old structures. When we look at urban development, restoring instead of razing not only maintains our cultural heritage but also promotes sustainability. It's a win-win in my books.

HOBBIES AND INTERESTS

1. What hobbies do you have in your free time?

5W1H Ideas:
Who: I
What: Engage in hobbies
When: During my free time
Where: At home or outdoors
Why: To relax and enjoy myself
How: Depending on the hobby, either alone or with friends

Answer: In my downtime, I often find myself indulging in photography and reading novels. While photography allows me to capture moments, reading transports me to different worlds.

2. How did you get started with your hobbies?

5W1H Ideas:
Who: I
What: Started my hobbies
When: A few years back
Where: At home or during travels
Why: Out of curiosity or influence from friends
How: Picked up a camera or a book and gave it a try

Answer: A few years ago, a close friend introduced me to the wonders of photography, and I was instantly hooked. As for reading, I remember picking up a mystery novel as a teen, and there was no looking back.

3. Are there any new hobbies you'd like to take up?

5W1H Ideas:
Who: I
What: Wish to take up new hobbies
When: In the near future
Where: Depending on the hobby
Why: To learn something new or challenge myself
How: Joining a class or self-learning

Answer: Lately, I've been toying with the idea of learning a musical instrument, perhaps the guitar. It's always fascinated me, and I think it would be a great way to challenge myself.

4. Do your friends share the same hobbies as you?

5W1H Ideas:
Who: My friends
What: Share or not share the same hobbies
When: In our conversations or hangouts
Where: Various settings like at home, cafes, or during trips
Why: Because hobbies are common topics of discussion
How: Through discussions or joint activities

Answer: A handful of my friends are avid readers like me, but when it comes to photography, not many have taken a keen interest. However, it's always a treat when our hobbies overlap, making our hangouts even more special.

5. How often do you indulge in your hobbies?

5W1H Ideas:
Who: I
What: Indulge in my hobbies
When: Mostly during weekends
Where: At home or specific hobby-related venues
Why: To take a break and refresh my mind
How: By dedicating specific time or being spontaneous

Answer: Most weekends, you'll find me with a camera in hand or buried in a good book. It's my way of unwinding and taking a breather from the week's chaos.

6. Do you prefer indoor or outdoor hobbies?

5W1H Ideas:
Who: I
What: Have a preference for indoor or outdoor hobbies
When: During leisure times
Where: Either indoors or outdoors
Why: Based on mood or the type of hobby
How: Choose based on the activity's requirements or personal liking

Answer: While I cherish the tranquility of indoor hobbies like reading, there's something invigorating about outdoor activities like hiking. It really depends on my mood.

7. Have you ever turned a hobby into a profession?

5W1H Ideas:
Who: I
What: Turned or thought of turning a hobby into a profession
When: In the past or currently considering
Where: At my workplace or as an independent venture
Why: Passion and interest in the hobby
How: By enhancing skills and seeking opportunities

Answer: Although I've always loved photography, I've never taken the leap to turn it professional. However, the thought has crossed my mind a time or two!

8. How do you find new hobbies or interests?

5W1H Ideas:
Who: I
What: Discover new hobbies or interests
When: Occasionally
Where: Online, through friends, or experiences
Why: To try something new or diversify my leisure activities
How: Research, recommendations, or spontaneous exploration

Answer: Mostly, it's through friends' recommendations or stumbling upon something online. I believe in keeping the doors of curiosity wide open.

9. Are there any hobbies you've given up? Why?

5W1H Ideas:
Who: I
What: Gave up certain hobbies
When: Over the years
Where: Varies depending on the hobby
Why: Lack of time, interest change, or other priorities
How: Gradually reduced time spent on it until it stopped

Answer: I used to paint quite a bit in my younger days, but with time and shifting priorities, the brushes have found a quiet corner in my room.

10. How has the pandemic affected your hobbies?

5W1H Ideas:
Who: I
What: Experienced changes in hobbies due to the pandemic
When: During the past couple of years
Where: At home, primarily
Why: Restrictions, more free time, or personal growth
How: Adapted, discovered new hobbies, or deepened existing ones

Answer: The pandemic gave me more indoor time, so I rekindled my love for reading. But it also opened the door to new hobbies like baking.

HOME (ACCOMMODATION)

1. Where do you currently live?

5W1H Ideas:
Who: I
What: Live in a specific type of accommodation
When: Currently
Where: The location or type of area
Why: Work, family, or personal reasons
How: Rented, owned, or shared

Answer: I currently reside in a cozy apartment in the heart of the city, mainly because it's close to my workplace.

2. Can you describe your home?

5W1H Ideas:
Who: I
What: Live in a specific home
When: Since a certain year or time
Where: Specific location or setting
Why: Personal preferences or circumstances
How: The features or characteristics of the home

Answer: Certainly! I dwell in a spacious two-bedroom flat that boasts large windows and a balcony with a stunning view of the park.

3. What's your favorite room in your home?

5W1H Ideas:
Who: I
What: Have a favorite room
When: Whenever I spend time there
Where: In my house
Why: Comfort, utility, or personal liking
How: Decor, utilities, or memories associated

Answer: I absolutely adore the living room. It's the heart of the home where family gatherings happen, and the décor gives it a warm, welcoming vibe.

4. How long have you lived there?

5W1H Ideas:
Who: I
What: Have been living in the current home
When: From a specific time or year
Where: The current residence
Why: Various reasons like work or family
How: Continuous residence or with breaks

Answer: I've called this place home for about five years now. Moved here due to its proximity to my office.

5. Are there any changes you'd like to make to your home?

5W1H Ideas:
Who: I
What: Wish to make certain changes
When: In the near future or someday
Where: In my current home
Why: Aesthetic, comfort, or utility reasons
How: Renovations, redecorations, or additions

Answer: Oh, definitely! I've been mulling over revamping the kitchen. A modern touch with some extra storage space would be a dream come true.

6. Is your home close to the city center?

5W1H Ideas:
Who: My home
What: Located at a certain distance
When: Currently
Where: In relation to the city center
Why: Chose this location or happened to be there
How: By walking, driving, or public transport

Answer: Yes, my home is a stone's throw away from the city center. It's super convenient for shopping and work.

7. What do you see when you look out of your window?

5W1H Ideas:
Who: I
What: See specific views or scenes
When: Whenever I look out
Where: From my window
Why: Because of the home's location
How: Observing or noticing

Answer: Every time I gaze out, I'm greeted by the bustling city streets and the distant silhouette of the mountains. It's a blend of urban and natural.

8. What kind of neighbors do you have?

5W1H Ideas:
Who: My neighbors
What: Are of a certain type or character
When: Currently
Where: Next to or around my home
Why: By chance or selection of the area
How: Their behavior or interactions with me

Answer: My neighbors are a mixed bag – some young families, a few elderly couples, and a lively bunch of college students. It's a harmonious blend.

9. How would you improve your living space?

5W1H Ideas:
Who: I
What: Would make certain improvements
When: If I had the resources or time
Where: In my living space
Why: For better aesthetics or functionality
How: By adding or changing certain things

Answer: I'd love to sprinkle a bit of greenery with indoor plants and maybe add some artwork. It'd make the space feel livelier and more personalized.

10. Is there anything you dislike about your current home?

5W1H Ideas:
Who: I
What: Dislike certain aspects
When: Since I've been living there
Where: In my current home
Why: Due to personal preferences or issues faced
How: Experience or comparison with other homes

Answer: To be honest, I wish the rooms had better natural lighting. Sometimes, it feels a tad bit gloomy on overcast days.

LANGUAGES AND COMMUNICATION

1. How many languages can you speak?

5W1H Ideas:
Who: I
What: Speak a certain number of languages
When: Over the course of my life
Where: Depending on the setting or country
Why: Due to education, heritage, or
personal interest
How: Learning through school, courses, or
immersion

Answer: Throughout my journey, I've managed to pick up three languages. English, Punjabi, and a smattering of French, mainly through school and travels.

2. What was the first language you learned?

5W1H Ideas:
Who: I
What: Learned a specific language first
When: As a child
Where: At home or in school
Why: It being my native language or due to
my surroundings
How: Through conversations and formal lessons

Answer: Punjabi was the first language I was introduced to, being the common tongue spoken at home and in our community.

3. Do you think it's important to learn a new language?

5W1H Ideas:
Who: Everyone/individuals
What: Learn new languages
When: In the modern globalized era
Where: Worldwide
Why: For communication, opportunities, or
personal growth
How: By breaking cultural barriers and
enhancing understanding

Answer: Absolutely, in this global village, picking up a new language is more than just communication; it's a bridge to understanding diverse cultures.

4. How did you learn English?

5W1H Ideas:
Who: I
What: Learned English
When: Starting in school
Where: In school and through various media
Why: As an essential language and
curriculum requirement
How: Through rigorous classes, practice,
and real-life interactions

Answer: I honed my English skills primarily in school. Of course, movies, books, and daily conversations played a pivotal role too.

5. Do you often communicate with people who speak a different language?

5W1H Ideas:
Who: I
What: Communicate with speakers of other languages
When: Occasionally or frequently
Where: In various settings, possibly work or travel
Why: Due to diverse interactions or requirements
How: Using English or a mutual language as a bridge

Answer: Yes, in the melting pot of our global society, I often find myself conversing with those who have a different native tongue, usually resorting to English.

6. Is there a language you'd love to learn in the future?

5W1H Ideas:
Who: I
What: Desire to learn a new language - spanish
When: In the foreseeable future
Where: Potentially through a course or self-study
Why: Due to interest, work, or travel plans
How: By dedicating time and effort

Answer: I've always been fascinated by Spanish. Someday, I aim to enroll in a course and embrace the language, especially given its widespread use.

7. How often do you practice speaking English?

5W1H Ideas:
Who: I
What: Practice speaking English
When: Regularly or occasionally
Where: At work, school, or in social settings
Why: To maintain fluency and confidence
How: Engaging in discussions, reading aloud, or formal practice

Answer: I make it a point to practice English daily, be it at work, with friends, or even by narrating stories to myself.

8. Are there any challenges you face when learning a new language?

5W1H Ideas:
Who: I/every learner
What: Encounter challenges
When: During the language learning process
Where: In class, during self-study, or while practicing
Why: Due to differences in structure, sound, or grammar
How: By struggling with pronunciation, understanding, or memory

Answer: Every language has its quirks. Personally, grasping the right pronunciation is often a tongue-twister for me, especially with unfamiliar sounds.

9. Do you use any apps or tools to improve your language skills?

5W1H Ideas:
Who: I
What: Use apps/tools
When: As part of my regular study routine
Where: On my smartphone or computer
Why: To enhance language proficiency
How: By engaging in interactive lessons or exercises

Answer: Indeed, I lean on a few apps for brushing up my language prowess. They make learning so interactive and handy, especially on-the-go.

10. How do you feel when you communicate in a language you're still learning?

5W1H Ideas:
Who: I
What: Feel a certain emotion
When: While speaking a non-native language
Where: In varied settings
Why: Due to potential mistakes or lack of fluency
How: With hesitance, excitement, or pride

Answer: It's a mix of exhilaration and nerves. While I'm thrilled to put what I've learned into play, there's always that fear of making a faux pas.

LEISURE ACTIVITIES

1. What leisure activity do you enjoy most on weekends?

5W1H Ideas:
Who: I
What: Engage in a leisure activity
When: On weekends
Where: At a specific place or home
Why: For relaxation or fun
How: Alone or with friends

Answer: Every weekend, I eagerly embrace hiking. Exploring new trails in the outskirts with my close friends is truly invigorating. This activity is my perfect escape from the weekly grind.

2. How much time do you dedicate to hobbies daily?

5W1H Ideas:
Who: I
What: Spend time on hobbies
When: Daily
Where: At home or a specific location
Why: To unwind and refresh my mind
How: Consistently, setting aside specific hours

Answer: Daily, I carve out an hour, immersing myself in painting. Whether at home or in a nearby park, it's my tranquil retreat, offering a refreshing break from routine.

3. Are there leisure activities you wish to try?

5W1H Ideas:
Who: I
What: Desire to attempt new activities
When: In the near future
Where: Various locations depending on the activity
Why: Sparked by curiosity or friends' recommendations
How: By joining workshops or groups

Answer: I've got a growing itch to venture into kayaking. Friends' tales of their exhilarating experiences fuel this desire. I'm scouting for the perfect beginner's workshop.

4. How often do you indulge in movies for leisure?

5W1H Ideas:
Who: I
What: Watch movies
When: Often, especially weekends
Where: Mostly at home, occasionally in cinemas
Why: To relax and entertain myself
How: By choosing based on recommendations or moods

Answer: Movies are my frequent weekend companions. I cherish those hours, lounging at home with a classic film or occasionally treating myself to the cinema's ambiance.

5. Do you prefer outdoor or indoor leisure activities?

5W1H Ideas:
Who: I
What: Have a preference for types of leisure activities
When: During free time
Where: Either outdoors or indoors
Why: Based on comfort, experience, or mood
How: Choosing based on environment and interest

Answer: I lean towards outdoor activities, especially when the weather's inviting. Feeling the fresh air while engaged in a hobby simply amplifies the joy.

6. Is there a popular leisure activity in your city?

5W1H Ideas:
Who: Locals in my city
What: Engage in a popular leisure activity
When: Especially on weekends or holidays
Where: Across the city
Why: Maybe it's culturally ingrained or trendy
How: Participating in groups or individually

Answer: In my city, weekend picnics at local parks are the rage. Families, friends, everyone seems to bask in the sun, making the most of their day.

7. Are you a fan of any sport?

5W1H Ideas:
Who: I
What: Fond of a specific sport
When: Whenever matches occur
Where: On TV or sometimes live
Why: Admiration for the game or players
How: Watching, discussing, or sometimes playing

Answer: Cricket has always held a special place in my heart. Be it watching nail-biting matches or discussing them later, it's always a thrill.

8. How do you usually spend your evenings?

5W1H Ideas:
Who: I
What: Spend my evenings
When: Every day
Where: Home or occasionally out
Why: To unwind after a day's work
How: Engaging in specific activities or relaxation

Answer: My evenings are reserved for tranquility. I often find solace with a good book, immersed in tales till nightfall.

9. Do you enjoy group activities or solo ones more?

5W1H Ideas:
Who: I
What: Engage in leisure activities
When: During free time
Where: Various locations depending on the activity
Why: Preference based on comfort or mood
How: Either solo or in a group

Answer: There's a charm in solo endeavors, giving me space to reflect. However, group activities often bring laughter and shared memories, which I equally cherish.

10. Which leisure activity helps you relax the most?

5W1H Ideas:
Who: I
What: Find relaxation in a specific activity
When: Whenever stressed or in need of relaxation
Where: At a comfortable spot, usually home
Why: To de-stress and rejuvenate
How: Engaging in the activity mindfully

Answer: Music is my sanctuary. Whenever life gets overwhelming, I plug in my headphones and let melodies wash over me.

LOCAL ATTRACTIONS

1. Are there many tourist attractions in your town?

5W1H Ideas:
Who: Tourists and locals
What: Visit tourist attractions
When: Throughout the year
Where: In my town
Why: To experience and appreciate local culture and beauty
How: By exploring different sites

Answer: Indeed, my town is blessed with a plethora of tourist attractions. Both locals and visitors flock to these spots, whether it's to absorb history, enjoy scenic beauty, or immerse in cultural events. Each site tells its own unique story.

2. What's the most famous attraction near your place?

5W1H Ideas:
Who: Tourists primarily
What: Visit the famous attraction
When: Especially during peak seasons
Where: Near my residence
Why: Its fame and significance
How: By touring and sometimes guided visits

Answer: The most renowned attraction near my home is the majestic 'Golden Fort'. Its imposing structure, intertwined with tales of valor and romance, draws countless tourists annually. The intricate architecture and historical significance make it an unforgettable visit.

3. Do you think it's important for a city to have tourist spots?

5W1H Ideas:
Who: City officials and residents
What: Maintain and promote tourist spots
When: Consistently
Where: Within the city
Why: To attract tourists and boost the economy
How: Through development, maintenance, and marketing

Answer: Absolutely! Tourist spots not only showcase a city's heritage and culture but also bolster its economy. They bring in visitors, which leads to job opportunities, cultural exchanges, and promotes the city on a global stage. It's a win-win for everyone.

4. How often do you visit local attractions?

5W1H Ideas:
Who: I
What: Visit local attractions
When: Occasionally
Where: Around the town
Why: To unwind, enjoy, or show around friends
How: Mostly on weekends or holidays

Answer: I frequent local attractions every now and then, especially when friends or family from out-of-town visit. It's always a joy rediscovering the charm of my own city, reminiscing old memories, and creating new ones.

5. Are there any historical sites in your city?

5W1H Ideas:
Who: History enthusiasts and tourists
What: Explore historical sites
When: Anytime during the year
Where: In my city
Why: To delve into the past and appreciate history
How: Visiting and often with the help of guides

Answer: Yes, our city boasts several historical sites, each echoing tales from the past. The grandeur of ancient monuments and ruins captures the imagination, transporting visitors back in time. Whenever I'm there, I feel deeply connected to our city's rich tapestry of history.

6. Do locals visit these attractions as often as tourists?

5W1H Ideas:
Who: Locals and tourists
What: Visit the attractions
When: Throughout the year
Where: In the city's attractions
Why: Locals for relaxation and tourists for exploration
How: On weekends or during special events

Answer: While tourists regularly flock to these attractions to explore and discover, locals also visit, albeit less frequently. They often come during weekends or special events, seeking a leisurely break or to revisit familiar spots, contrasting the novelty tourists seek.

7. Is there a local spot that's not well-known but should be?

5W1H Ideas:
Who: Locals primarily
What: Visit the lesser-known spot
When: Usually in their free time
Where: Hidden within the city
Why: Because of its unique charm and tranquility
How: Often by word of mouth or local recommendations

Answer: Certainly, there's a serene garden hidden in the city's heart that many locals cherish but remains lesser-known to tourists. Its tranquility offers an escape from urban chaos. While it's our little secret, its charm certainly deserves wider recognition.

8. What activities can visitors do at these tourist spots?

5W1H Ideas:
Who: Visitors and tourists
What: Engage in various activities
When: During their visit
Where: At the tourist spots
Why: To enhance their experience and enjoyment
How: Through guided tours, workshops, or self-exploration

Answer: Visitors can dive deep into a myriad of activities at these spots. From guided historical tours to hands-on workshops, and even leisurely picnics or boat rides, there's something for everyone. These activities truly elevate the entire tourist experience.

9. How do these attractions impact the local economy?

5W1H Ideas:
Who: Local businesses and the community
What: Benefit from the attractions
When: Especially during peak tourist seasons
Where: In and around the attractions
Why: Due to increased footfall and tourist expenditure
How: By offering services, goods, and experiences

Answer: These attractions significantly boost the local economy. Especially during peak seasons, businesses thrive as tourists spend on accommodation, food, souvenirs, and experiences. The increased footfall invigorates the entire community, leading to job creation and economic growth.

10. Are there any cultural events held near these attractions?

5W1H Ideas:
Who: Event organizers and the local community
What: Host cultural events
When: Annually or during specific seasons
Where: At or near the attractions
Why: To showcase local culture and traditions
How: Through festivals, performances, and exhibitions

Answer: Yes, cultural events are frequently held near these attractions, celebrating our rich traditions. Whether it's a festive fair, traditional dance performances, or art exhibitions, these events beautifully complement the attraction's essence, offering a deeper dive into our culture.

LOCAL TRADITIONS

1. What are some local traditions unique to your region?

5W1H Ideas:
Who: Locals in my region
What: Observe and celebrate unique traditions
When: On specific dates or seasons
Where: Throughout the region
Why: To honor history, culture, and ancestral customs
How: Through celebrations, rituals, and events

Answer: In our region, we have an array of distinctive traditions. For instance, every autumn, locals gather for the 'Harvest Dance Festival,' celebrating the season's bounty. These traditions, deeply rooted in our history and culture, offer glimpses into our shared heritage.

2. How often do you personally participate in these traditions?

5W1H Ideas:
Who: I
What: Participate in local traditions
When: As they occur, annually or seasonally
Where: In local settings or community centers
Why: To connect with my roots and community
How: Actively, by attending or even organizing

Answer: I make it a point to participate in these traditions whenever they occur, be it annually or seasonally. It's a way for me to reconnect with my roots and strengthen my bond with the community. Engaging in them feels like a journey back in time.

3. Do younger generations show interest in these traditions?

5W1H Ideas:
Who: Younger generations
What: Show interest or engage in traditions
When: During traditional events or celebrations
Where: In schools, homes, or community spaces
Why: To learn, connect, or out of curiosity
How: By participating, observing, or through educational programs

Answer: The younger generation indeed displays curiosity about these traditions. Schools and community centers often hold workshops or events, igniting interest and ensuring these age-old customs continue to resonate with the youth.

4. How have local traditions evolved over the years?

5W1H Ideas:
Who: The local community
What: Witness and adapt local traditions
When: Over generations and years
Where: Across the region
Why: Due to changing times, influences, or modernization
How: By blending the old with new elements or practices

Answer: Local traditions have witnessed an evolution, blending ancestral customs with contemporary elements. While the essence remains unchanged, modern influences, be it in music, attire, or even food, have woven into these traditions, making them ever-evolving and vibrant.

5. Are there any local traditions that are exclusively practiced by certain groups within the community?

5W1H Ideas:
Who: Specific groups within the community
What: Practice exclusive traditions
When: On certain occasions or dates
Where: In their group settings or special places
Why: To honor their specific history or beliefs
How: Through private ceremonies, rituals, or gatherings

Answer: Yes, certain groups within our community have their unique traditions. For instance, the 'Mountain Clan' celebrates the 'Moonlight Ritual' every spring. These traditions, exclusive to their lineage, add layers of depth and diversity to our broader cultural tapestry.

6. Do people in your town wear traditional outfits on special occasions?

5W1H Ideas:
Who: People in my town
What: Wear traditional outfits
When: On special occasions or festivals
Where: At events, family gatherings, or community celebrations
Why: To honor the tradition and show cultural pride
How: By donning specific clothes associated with the occasion

Answer: Absolutely, during special occasions, many locals wear traditional attire, showcasing our rich heritage. It's a delightful sight to see streets filled with colorful and historically significant outfits, especially during festivals.

7. Are there any traditional songs or dances in your locality?

5W1H Ideas:
Who: Residents of my locality
What: Perform traditional songs and dances
When: During festivals, weddings, or local events
Where: Community halls, open grounds, or at homes
Why: Celebrate, keep the culture alive, and entertain
How: By teaching the younger generation and through live performances

Answer: Yes, there are. Traditional songs and dances like bhangra, giddha are integral to our local culture. These melodies and movements are passed down generations, ensuring they remain alive and continue to enchant attendees during various occasions.

8. How do local traditions influence the daily life of people in your area?

5W1H Ideas:
Who: The locals
What: Get influenced by local traditions
When: In daily activities or during specific times of the year
Where: At homes, workplaces, and community spaces
Why: Uphold values, beliefs, and cultural identity
How: Through practices, rituals, or lifestyle choices

Answer: Local traditions significantly shape our daily lives, instilling values and guiding our actions. From the food we eat to the festivals we celebrate; these traditions offer a framework for our community's shared identity.

9. Are there traditional crafts or arts that are popular in your region?

5W1H Ideas:
Who: Artisans and residents
What: Create and appreciate traditional crafts and arts
When: All year round
Where: Local markets, homes, and workshops
Why: Preserve cultural identity and for economic reasons
How: By crafting, selling, and passing on the skills

Answer: Certainly, our region is known for its exquisite pottery and weaving. Artisans passionately craft these, and they're not just beautiful but also reflect the soul and history of our community. Many households proudly display these as a nod to our roots.

10. Do schools in your area teach about local traditions?

5W1H Ideas:
Who: Schools and educators
What: Teach about local traditions
When: Throughout the academic year
Where: In schools and educational institutions
Why: Educate the young generation about their heritage
How: Through curriculum, events, or special classes

Answer: Yes, schools place emphasis on imparting knowledge about our local traditions. It's a means to bridge the past with the present, ensuring students understand and appreciate the legacy they inherit. Special events and classes often celebrate this heritage

MUSIC AND CONCERTS

1. Do you often listen to music?

5W1H Ideas:
Who: I
What: Listen to music
When: Often, during various times of the day
Where: At home, while commuting, or at work
Why: For relaxation, entertainment, or concentration
How: Using headphones, speakers, or attending live events

Answer: Yes, I frequently listen to music. It's a daily ritual for me, be it during my commute, work breaks, or while unwinding at home. It's a source of relaxation and joy for me.

2. What type of music do you prefer?

5W1H Ideas:
Who: I
What: Have a preference for certain types of music
When: Whenever I listen to music
Where: Regardless of location
Why: Personal taste and mood
How: By choosing specific genres or artists

Answer: I gravitate towards soft rock and indie genres. They resonate with my mood and taste, offering a soothing backdrop to my day.

3. Have you ever been to a live concert?

5W1H Ideas:
Who: I
What: Attended a live concert
When: In the past
Where: At concert venues
Why: Experience live music and the ambiance
How: Buying tickets and going with friends

Answer: Yes, I've attended a few live concerts. The experience is electrifying, and feeling the music reverberate through a crowd is unmatched.

4. Do you play any musical instruments?

5W1H Ideas:
Who: I
What: Play musical instruments
When: Occasionally or during free time
Where: At home or in classes
Why: Passion, hobby, or learning
How: Self-taught or through lessons

Answer: I dabble with the guitar. Picked it up as a hobby a few years back. It's a wonderful way for me to express myself and relax.

5. Is there a popular music genre in your country?

5W1H Ideas:
Who: People in my country
What: Listen to a popular music genre
When: Currently or in recent years
Where: Across the nation
Why: Cultural influence or modern trends
How: Radio, streaming services, or live performances

Answer: Absolutely, pop music holds a significant place in my country. It's widely played on radios, and many artists have a massive following.

6. How often do you discover new music?

5W1H Ideas:
Who: I
What: Discover new music
When: Regularly, whenever I explore
Where: Online streaming platforms, recommendations from friends
Why: To diversify my playlist and stay updated
How: Browsing, recommendations, or curated playlists

Answer: I regularly explore new music, especially on streaming platforms. It keeps my playlist fresh and introduces me to different artists and genres.

7. Do you have a favorite song right now?

5W1H Ideas:
Who: I
What: Have a favorite song
When: Currently
Where: On my playlist, in my mind
Why: Resonates with my feelings or simply catchy
How: Listening on repeat

Answer: Yes, I've been playing one song, masoomiyat by Satinder Sartaj, on repeat lately. It's catchy and perfectly captures my current mood.

8. Is there any music you don't like listening to?

5W1H Ideas:
Who: I
What: Avoid certain types of music
When: Whenever I come across it
Where: On the radio, playlists, etc.
Why: Doesn't appeal to my taste
How: Skip the track or change the station

Answer: Certainly, heavy metal doesn't sit well with my musical taste. I tend to skip such tracks when they play.

9. Did your music preferences change over the years?

5W1H Ideas:
Who: I
What: Had a change in music preferences
When: Over the years
Where: In terms of music genres and artists
Why: Exposure to new genres, life experiences, or maturity
How: Gradual shift in the type of music I enjoy

Answer: Definitely, my preferences evolved. While I loved pop in my teens, I've grown fond of classical and jazz as I matured.

10. How do you usually listen to music?

5W1H Ideas:
Who: I
What: Listen to music
When: During various activities or free time
Where: Home, gym, commuting
Why: To relax, energize, or accompany tasks
How: Via phone, computer, or live

Answer: I primarily use my phone to stream music. Whether I'm working out, commuting, or simply chilling, it's always within arm's reach.

MUSEUMS AND GALLERIES

1. Do you often visit museums or art galleries?

5W1H Ideas:
Who: I
What: Visit museums and art galleries
When: Occasionally, on weekends or holidays
Where: In my city or when traveling
Why: To appreciate art and learn about history
How: Alone or with friends

Answer: Occasionally, I take time on weekends to visit museums and galleries in my city. It's a wonderful way to delve into art and history.

2. Which was the last museum you went to?

5W1H Ideas:
Who: I
What: Went to a museum
When: Last month
Where: In the downtown area of my city
Why: To see a special exhibition
How: With a group of friends

Answer: Last month, I visited a museum downtown with some friends. We were particularly excited about a special exhibition they were hosting.

3. Do you prefer art galleries or history museums?

5W1H Ideas:
Who: I
What: Have a preference between art galleries and history museums
When: Whenever I choose to visit
Where: Depending on the exhibits
Why: Personal interest and the kind of experience I seek
How: Based on my mood and interest

Answer: I have a slight inclination towards art galleries. The visual appeal and emotions behind artworks intrigue me more than historical artifacts.

4. Are there any famous museums in your city?

5W1H Ideas:
Who: My city
What: Houses famous museums
When: Established over the years
Where: Different parts of the city
Why: To preserve and showcase art and history
How: Funded by the government or private entities

Answer: Yes, my city boasts a couple of renowned museums that attract visitors from all over. They beautifully encapsulate our region's art and history. One of them is the Sikh Museum, just a stone throw away from my village.

5. Would you buy a painting from a gallery?

5W1H Ideas:
Who: I
What: Buy a painting
When: If I find something captivating
Where: From an art gallery
Why: To adorn my living space and support artists
How: Depending on its appeal and my budget

Answer: If a painting truly captivates me and fits my budget, I'd definitely consider buying it from a gallery. It's a blend of personal aesthetics and supporting the arts.

6. How important are museums for education?

5W1H Ideas:
Who: Museums
What: Play a role in education
When: For school trips or individual visits
Where: Across the world
Why: They are repositories of knowledge and culture
How: Through exhibits, workshops, and guided tours

Answer: Museums play a pivotal role in education. They offer a tangible connection to our past and present, providing a hands-on learning experience that books often can't.

7. Are most museums in your country free to enter?

5W1H Ideas:
Who: Museums in my country
What: Charge an entrance fee or offer free admission
When: On specific days or always
Where: Across the country
Why: To maintain the facility or promote culture
How: Government funding or ticket sales

Answer: In my country, several museums have an entrance fee, but there are also quite a few that offer free admission, especially on special occasions.

8. How often did you visit museums as a child?

5W1H Ideas:
Who: I, as a child
What: Visited museums
When: Mostly during school trips or family outings
Where: Local museums or those in neighboring cities
Why: To learn and explore
How: With schoolmates or family

Answer: As a child, I mostly visited museums during school trips or occasional family outings. It was a blend of fun and learning.

9. Do you think art galleries are more for adults than children?

5W1H Ideas:
Who: Art galleries
What: Appeal to a certain age group
When: During visits
Where: Globally
Why: Due to the nature of art or the understanding required
How: Through the content displayed

Answer: I believe art galleries can be appreciated by all age groups. However, some artworks might resonate more with adults due to their themes or nuances.

10. Have you ever taken a guided tour in a museum?

5W1H Ideas:
Who: I
What: Took a guided tour
When: During one of my visits
Where: In a particular museum
Why: To get detailed insights into the exhibits
How: Led by a knowledgeable guide

Answer: Yes, I've taken a guided tour in a museum. It was enlightening as the guide provided deeper insights into the exhibits and their significance.

NATURE AND ENVIRONMENT

1. Do you like spending time outdoors?

5W1H Ideas:
Who: I
What: Enjoy spending time outdoors
When: Especially during weekends or holidays
Where: In parks, gardens, or countryside
Why: To rejuvenate and connect with nature
How: Often alone or with friends and family

Answer: Absolutely, I cherish spending time outdoors. Whether it's the weekend or a holiday, being in a park or garden refreshes my mind and spirits.

2. What's your favorite season?

5W1H Ideas:
Who: I
What: Have a favorite season
When: Year-round
Where: In my country
Why: Due to the weather, activities, or festivals
How: Naturally occurring

Answer: My favorite season has to be spring. Everything is so vibrant and alive, and the mild weather is just perfect for various activities.

3. Do you have many plants at home?

5W1H Ideas:
Who: I
What: Have plants
When: Currently
Where: At home, possibly in a garden or balcony
Why: To beautify space or for health benefits
How: Tending to them regularly

Answer: Yes, I have a collection of plants at home. They not only beautify the space but also bring a sense of tranquility.

4. How do you feel about zoos?

5W1H Ideas:
Who: I
What: My opinion on zoos
When: Presently
Where: Globally
Why: Due to animal rights concerns or educational value
How: Based on personal experiences or knowledge

Answer: I have mixed feelings about zoos. While they play an educational role, I also ponder about the well-being of animals in captivity.

5. Is recycling popular in your hometown?

5W1H Ideas:
Who: People in my hometown
What: Practice recycling
When: Nowadays
Where: In my hometown
Why: To protect the environment and reduce waste
How: Through designated bins or recycling centers

Answer: Yes, recycling has gained momentum in my hometown. People are increasingly conscious about environmental protection and actively participate in recycling programs.

6. Do you prefer the countryside or the city?

5W1H Ideas:
Who: I
What: Preference between the countryside or the city
When: Generally, when choosing a place to live or visit
Where: In my country or abroad
Why: Due to peace and nature or amenities and hustle-bustle
How: Based on past experiences or aspirations

Answer: I have a soft spot for the countryside. The serenity and close connection to nature make it an ideal place for me to relax and rejuvenate.

7. Are there many parks or forests near your home?

5W1H Ideas:
Who: I
What: Live near parks or forests
When: Currently
Where: Around my residence
Why: Proximity to natural spots for recreation or relaxation
How: They are naturally present or designed by authorities

Answer: Yes, there's a beautiful park not too far from my home. It's a great spot for morning walks and offers a touch of nature amidst urban surroundings.

8. How often do you go for nature walks?

5W1H Ideas:
Who: I
What: Go for nature walks
When: Mostly during weekends or holidays
Where: In nearby parks, forests, or trails
Why: To exercise, relax, or connect with nature
How: Alone, with friends, or in guided groups

Answer: I try to go for nature walks during weekends. It's a refreshing way to exercise and, at the same time, stay connected with the natural world.

9. Do you believe it's important to teach children about nature?

5W1H Ideas:
Who: I
What: Believe in imparting nature education to children
When: During their formative years
Where: At home, school, or during trips
Why: To inculcate respect for the environment and awareness
How: Through direct experience, stories, or educational modules

Answer: Absolutely, I firmly believe children should learn about nature early on. It instills a sense of respect for the environment and helps them understand our planet's delicate balance.

10. What's your favorite natural landmark?

5W1H Ideas:
Who: I
What: Have a favorite natural landmark
When: From my travels or knowledge
Where: Could be anywhere in the world
Why: Due to its beauty, significance, or personal experience
How: Visited during a trip or learned about it

Answer: I'm particularly fond of the Grand Canyon. Its sheer magnitude and breathtaking beauty left an indelible mark on me during my visit.

NEWS AND CURRENT EVENTS

1. How do you usually get your news?

5W1H Ideas:
Who: I
What: Obtain news updates
When: Daily or whenever major events occur
Where: From various sources
Why: To stay informed
How: Through TV, newspapers, online platforms, etc.

Answer: I typically get my news from online sources, checking updates on my phone. It's quick and I can read them on the go.

2. Do you prefer reading newspapers or watching news on TV?

5W1H Ideas:
Who: I
What: Preference between newspapers or TV news
When: When consuming daily news
Where: At home or elsewhere
Why: Based on convenience, reliability, or personal preference
How: Sitting in the living room or browsing on the commute

Answer: I lean towards reading newspapers. I enjoy the detailed analysis, and it allows me to read at my own pace.

3. How important is it for you to stay updated with current events?

5W1H Ideas:
Who: I
What: Feel about staying updated with news
When: In today's fast-paced world
Where: In my country and globally
Why: To be aware, make informed decisions, or for general knowledge
How: By actively seeking news or discussing with peers

Answer: It's quite essential for me to stay updated. Knowing what's happening around the world helps me make informed decisions and contributes to my general awareness.

4. Are there specific types of news that interest you more?

5W1H Ideas:
Who: I
What: Have a particular interest in certain news genres
When: Whenever they are broadcasted or published
Where: In various news outlets
Why: Due to personal interest, relevance, or curiosity
How: Actively searching or following dedicated segments

Answer: Yes, I'm especially drawn to technological advancements and science news. The rapid pace of innovation fascinates me.

5. Do you discuss current events with your friends or family?

5W1H Ideas:
Who: I, with friends or family
What: Discuss current events
When: During gatherings, meals, or casual conversations
Where: At home, work, or social gatherings
Why: To share opinions, stay informed, or ignite discussions
How: Casually or in more structured settings like debates

Answer: Quite often, yes. Discussing current events with friends and family not only keeps me informed but also offers diverse perspectives

6. Do you think newspapers will be out of fashion in the future?

5W1H Ideas:
Who: I
What: Predict the future of newspapers
When: In the foreseeable future
Where: Globally
Why: Due to the rise of digital media
How: The shift from traditional to online platforms

Answer: While digital news is on the rise, I believe newspapers have a certain charm and won't completely go out of fashion. There's something special about flipping through the pages of a physical newspaper.

7. How do you feel about fake news and its impact?

5W1H Ideas:
Who: I
What: Thoughts on the spread and impact of fake news
When: In the current digital age
Where: On social media and other platforms
Why: Due to potential misinformation and its consequences
How: Being vigilant and verifying news sources

Answer: Fake news is a real thorn in the side. It can mislead and cause unwarranted panic. It's crucial to double-check sources and not take everything at face value.

8. Do you ever feel overwhelmed by the constant flow of news?

5W1H Ideas:
Who: I
What: Feel about the continuous influx of news
When: In today's 24/7 news cycle
Where: Across all media platforms
Why: Due to the information overload
How: By taking breaks or limiting news consumption

Answer: Sometimes it feels like there's no escaping the news, especially with the 24/7 news cycle. Every now and then, I get a bit overwhelmed and need to switch off and take a breather.

9. Have you ever attended a news or media event in person?

5W1H Ideas:
Who: I
What: Attend a news-related event
When: Anytime in the past
Where: At a specific location or venue
Why: Interest, work, or other reasons
How: By getting an invitation, purchasing a ticket, etc.

Answer: Yes, I once went to a press conference about an upcoming event in town. It was quite an eye-opening experience, seeing how news is made behind the scenes.

10. Are there certain journalists or news anchors you particularly trust?

5W1H Ideas:
Who: I
What: Have trust in specific journalists or anchors
When: Whenever I watch or read the news
Where: On various news channels or publications
Why: Because of their credibility, style, or in-depth reporting
How: Over years of consistent and reliable news delivery

Answer: Definitely. There are a couple of journalists whose work I hold in high regard. They've always been on the ball, providing accurate and in-depth information.

PARKS AND OUTDOOR ACTIVITIES

1. Do you often visit parks or gardens?

5W1H Ideas:
Who: I
What: Visit parks or gardens
When: Frequently
Where: In the local area or during travels
Why: To relax, exercise, or enjoy nature
How: By walking, cycling, or using public transport

Answer: Yes, I often take a stroll in the local park. It's my way of getting a breath of fresh air and clearing my head after a long day.

2. What outdoor activities do you enjoy the most?

5W1H Ideas:
Who: I
What: Enjoy specific outdoor activities
When: On weekends or free days
Where: Parks, gardens, or other outdoor spaces
Why: For relaxation, exercise, or adventure
How: Alone, with friends, or in groups

Answer: I'm an avid hiker. Hitting the trails and soaking in the beauty of nature is like a walk in the park for me. It's both refreshing and invigorating.

3. Are there any outdoor sports you're keen on trying?

5W1H Ideas:
Who: I
What: Interested in trying new outdoor sports
When: In the future
Where: At suitable venues or locations
Why: For challenge, fun, or fitness
How: By joining a club or going with friends

Answer: I've always wanted to give rock climbing a shot. The idea of scaling heights and the adrenaline rush it brings sounds right up my alley.

4. How do you feel about picnics?

5W1H Ideas:
Who: I
What: Feelings about picnics
When: During suitable weather
Where: In parks or scenic spots
Why: For leisure, food, and company
How: By preparing food and gathering with loved ones

Answer: I think picnics are a piece of cake when it comes to bonding. It's a delightful way to connect with loved ones while enjoying a meal amidst nature.

5. Do parks in your city offer facilities for children or fitness enthusiasts?

5W1H Ideas:
Who: Parks in my city
What: Offer specific facilities
When: Throughout the year
Where: Across different parks
Why: For recreation, fitness, or children's play
How: By incorporating playgrounds, fitness zones, etc.

Answer: Absolutely, our local parks are no slouch when it comes to facilities. They boast children's playgrounds and designated areas with gym equipment for fitness buffs.

6. How often do you engage in outdoor physical activities?

5W1H Ideas:
Who: I
What: Engage in outdoor physical activities
When: Several times a week
Where: In parks, trails, or sports centers
Why: To maintain health and relieve stress
How: By jogging, cycling, or playing sports

Answer: I engage in outdoor physical activities several times a week. Whether it's jogging in the local park, cycling down trails, or playing sports at centers, I find it's an excellent way to maintain my health and take a breather from daily stress.

7. Do you prefer quiet parks or those bustling with activities?

5W1H Ideas:
Who: I
What: Preference for quiet or lively parks
When: During my visits
Where: Depending on the mood and occasion
Why: For solitude or socializing
How: By choosing specific parks

Answer: During my visits, I sometimes gravitate towards quiet parks for solitude and introspection. Other times, when I'm in the mood for a lively atmosphere, I opt for bustling ones to socialize and be part of activities.

8. Have you ever participated in a park event or festival?

5W1H Ideas:
Who: I
What: Participated in park events
When: On special occasions or festivals
Where: At local or city parks
Why: To celebrate, engage, or volunteer
How: By joining community groups or with friends

Answer: On special occasions, I've participated in park events. Whether it's at the local or city park, joining community groups or going with friends, I attend to celebrate, engage, and sometimes even volunteer.

9. What's your favorite time to visit the park?

5W1H Ideas:
Who: I
What: Visit the park
When: Preferably during mornings or evenings
Where: Local parks or gardens
Why: For fresh air, exercise, or relaxation
How: Usually on foot or by bicycle

Answer: I usually visit local parks or gardens during the mornings or evenings on foot or by bicycle. This preference stems from seeking fresh air, some exercise, or simply a moment of relaxation amidst nature.

10. How do parks benefit communities?

5W1H Ideas:
Who: Parks
What: Benefit communities
When: Throughout the year
Where: Across neighborhoods and cities
Why: Provide recreational spaces, improve health, and foster community bonding
How: By hosting events, providing facilities, and being accessible

Answer: Parks benefit communities throughout the year by providing recreational spaces across neighborhoods and cities. They host events, offer facilities, and remain accessible to all, playing pivotal roles in improving health and fostering community bonding.

PERSONAL ACHIEVEMENTS

1. Have you recently achieved something you're proud of?

5W1H Ideas:
Who: I
What: Achieved something noteworthy
When: Recently
Where: At work/school or personal life
Why: Due to hard work and perseverance
How: By staying focused and being committed

Answer: Recently, I did achieve something noteworthy in my personal life. After months of hard work and burning the midnight oil, I finally completed a marathon, a feat I never thought I'd accomplish.

2. Do you think it's essential to have goals in life?

5W1H Ideas:
Who: I
What: Importance of having goals
When: Throughout life's journey
Where: In personal and professional life
Why: To give direction and purpose
How: By setting benchmarks and pursuing them

Answer: Throughout life's journey, I firmly believe it's crucial to have goals, both in our personal and professional lives. They act as a compass, giving direction and purpose, ensuring we don't lose our way in the hustle and bustle.

3. What's the most challenging goal you've set for yourself?

5W1H Ideas:
Who: I
What: Set a challenging goal
When: In the past
Where: In a personal or professional context
Why: To push boundaries and grow
How: By aiming higher than usual

Answer: In the past, I set the bar high by aiming to master a new language within a year. It was a tall order, but it pushed my boundaries, allowing me to grow and learn in ways I hadn't anticipated.

4. How do you feel when you achieve a personal goal?

5W1H Ideas:
Who: I
What: Feelings after achieving a goal
When: Upon accomplishment
Where: Regardless of the setting
Why: Sense of fulfillment and pride
How: Through reflection and celebration

Answer: Upon achieving a personal goal, regardless of the setting, I feel on top of the world. There's an unmatched sense of fulfillment and pride that washes over me, making all the blood, sweat, and tears worth it.

5. Do you celebrate your achievements, big or small?

5W1H Ideas:
Who: I
What: Celebrate achievements
When: After accomplishing them
Where: At home or out with friends/family
Why: To acknowledge hard work
How: By treating myself or spending time with loved ones

Answer: Absolutely! After accomplishing any achievement, big or small, I make it a point to paint the town red. It's vital to acknowledge the hard work, whether by treating myself or spending quality time with loved ones.

6. Do you usually share your achievements with others?

5W1H Ideas:
Who: I
What: Sharing achievements
When: Right after achieving something
Where: With friends or family
Why: To spread happiness and gain motivation
How: Verbally or through social media

Answer: Yes, I do wear my heart on my sleeve when it comes to my achievements. Right after achieving something, I eagerly share it with friends and family, be it verbally or through social media. Their cheer gives me a shot in the arm.

7. How important is it for you to push your limits?

5W1H Ideas:
Who: I
What: Importance of pushing limits
When: Whenever facing challenges
Where: In all spheres of life
Why: To evolve and better oneself
How: By setting harder goals

Answer: For me, pushing the envelope is pivotal. Whenever I face challenges, I believe in setting harder goals and testing my waters. It's the best way to evolve and better oneself in this ever-changing world.

8. Has there been a time when you missed the mark on a personal goal?

5W1H Ideas:
Who: I
What: Missed achieving a goal
When: In the past
Where: Could be in studies or a hobby
Why: Due to unexpected hurdles or challenges
How: Despite best efforts

Answer: Yes, there have been times when, despite my best efforts, I've bitten off more than I could chew. Once, I aimed to read 50 books in a year but fell short due to unexpected hurdles. It was a humbling experience.

9. Do people around you support your ambitions?

5W1H Ideas:
Who: People around me
What: Support my ambitions
When: Throughout my journey
Where: In every endeavor
Why: They believe in me
How: By encouraging and guiding

Answer: Indeed, the people around me have always been my rock. Throughout my journey, they've stood by me like a pillar of strength, encouraging and guiding. It's heartwarming to know they've got my back.

10. Are there any achievements you're gunning for in the near future?

5W1H Ideas:
Who: I
What: Aiming for new achievements
When: In the near future
Where: Personal or professional arena
Why: Continuous growth and evolution
How: By planning and dedication

Answer: Absolutely! I've always been someone who doesn't rest on their laurels. In the near future, I'm setting my sights on some new goals in both my personal and professional life. Planning and dedication are the name of the game.

PERSONALITIES AND CHARACTERS

1. Do you think you're more introverted or extroverted?

5W1H Ideas:
Who: I
What: Being introverted or extroverted
When: Generally, in social situations
Where: At social gatherings or alone
Why: Natural inclination
How: Reacting to people and environments

Answer: I'd say I lean more towards being introverted. While I can be the life and soul of the party occasionally, I often find solace in my own company, recharging my batteries in a quiet environment.

2. How do your friends usually describe your personality?

5W1H Ideas:
Who: My friends
What: Describing my personality
When: When asked or discussing
Where: In casual conversations
Why: Share observations
How: By recalling experiences with me

Answer: My friends often say I'm as steady as a rock. They appreciate my calm demeanor, especially in the face of adversity. They also mention that I wear my heart on my sleeve, being transparent with my feelings.

3. Is there a personality trait you wish you had?

5W1H Ideas:
Who: I
What: Wishing for a specific trait
When: Sometimes, in reflective moments
Where: In certain situations where it's needed
Why: To handle situations differently
How: By observing others

Answer: Sometimes, I wish I had the gift of the gab. While I can communicate effectively, I admire those who can effortlessly charm their way through conversations and lighten up any room.

4. Do you believe personalities can change over time?

5W1H Ideas:
Who: People, in general
What: Changing personalities
When: Over the course of life
Where: Due to various life experiences
Why: Growth, experiences, and learning
How: By adapting and evolving

Answer: Certainly! I believe that as people go through the school of hard knocks, they adapt and evolve. Life experiences, both good and bad, mold our personalities in subtle ways.

5. Who in your life has a personality you truly admire?

5W1H Ideas:
Who: Someone close or known
What: Admirable personality
When: Since I've known them
Where: In various life situations
Why: Their unique traits and approach to life
How: By demonstrating consistent character

Answer: My grandmother has a personality I hold in high regard. She's been through thick and thin, yet her resilience and evergreen optimism are awe-inspiring. She truly marches to the beat of her own drum.

6. Are you more of a glass-half-full or glass-half-empty kind of person?

5W1H Ideas:
Who: I
What: Perspective on situations
When: When faced with challenges
Where: In daily life situations
Why: Inherent outlook on life
How: By interpreting situations

Answer: I've always been a glass-half-full individual. No matter the hurdles, I try to find the silver lining. It's just the way I've wired myself to see the world.

7. How do you handle stress or pressure?

5W1H Ideas:
Who: I
What: Handling stress or pressure
When: During challenging times
Where: At work, home, or in personal situations
Why: To maintain mental well-being
How: Using specific methods or techniques

Answer: When the going gets tough, I typically turn to meditation or a brisk walk. These helps clear my head and let me tackle challenges with a level head.

8. Are you often described as a morning person or a night owl?

5W1H Ideas:
Who: People who know me
What: Describing my active times
When: Based on daily routine
Where: Depending on my energy peaks
Why: Observing my productivity and energy
How: By noticing when I'm most alert

Answer: I'm definitely a morning person. As the saying goes, the early bird catches the worm. I feel most productive and energetic right after dawn.

9. How do you usually react when things don't go as planned?

5W1H Ideas:
Who: I
What: Reacting to unexpected situations
When: When things take a turn
Where: In various scenarios
Why: Natural reaction or learned response
How: By processing the situation

Answer: I tend to roll with the punches. While it's disappointing when things don't pan out, I believe every cloud has a silver lining. So, I adapt and look for the positive side.

10. Do you find it easy to mix and mingle in social situations?

5W1H Ideas:
Who: I
What: Interacting in social scenarios
When: At parties, gatherings, or events
Where: Social settings
Why: To engage and connect
How: Based on comfort and confidence

Answer: I wouldn't say I'm the life of the party, but I can hold my own in social settings. It's all about finding common ground and going with the flow.

PHOTOGRAPHY

1. Do you enjoy taking photographs?

5W1H Ideas:
Who: I
What: Taking photographs
When: On various occasions
Where: Everywhere I go
Why: For memories or creativity
How: Using a camera or phone

Answer: Absolutely! I believe a picture is worth a thousand words. Whether it's capturing memories or just admiring the beauty around, I enjoy snapping photos whenever I can.

2. How often do you click pictures with your phone?

5W1H Ideas:
Who: I
What: Clicking pictures
When: Quite often
Where: Anywhere, really
Why: Ease of the phone camera
How: Casually or for specific reasons

Answer: I'd say I'm quite snap-happy with my phone. It's so convenient that I find myself taking photos almost every day, be it of scenic views, friends, or just random moments.

3. Do you have a favorite type of photography, like landscapes or portraits?

5W1H Ideas:
Who: I
What: Preferred type of photography
When: Depending on the situation
Where: Various locations or setups
Why: Personal preference
How: By focusing on specific subjects

Answer: I've always been drawn to landscape photography. There's something about capturing the vast beauty of nature that really resonates with me. As they say, every picture tells a story.

4. Have you ever thought of taking up photography as a hobby or profession?

5W1H Ideas:
Who: I
What: Considering photography seriously
When: At times when I'm inspired
Where: After seeing professional works
Why: Passion for the art
How: Through courses or self-learning

Answer: I've toyed with the idea, especially when I'm in the zone and everything just clicks. But for now, it remains a passionate hobby. Who knows what the future holds, right?

5. Do you prefer taking candid shots or posed photographs?

5W1H Ideas:
Who: I
What: Types of shots
When: During events or casual moments
Where: Parties, outdoors, or casual gatherings
Why: For authentic moments or composed portraits
How: By waiting for natural reactions or giving directions

Answer: I lean more towards candid shots. They say the camera never lies, and I think candid photos capture the raw, genuine moments which make memories truly special.

6. How do you feel about sharing your photographs on social media?

5W1H Ideas:
Who: I
What: Sharing photos
When: After taking a good shot
Where: On social media platforms
Why: For sharing with friends or getting feedback
How: By posting with or without captions

Answer: I'm on the fence about it. While it's great to share memories and get feedback, I also believe some moments are best kept private. I guess it's about striking the right balance.

7. Do you ever edit your photos before showing them to others?

5W1H Ideas:
Who: I
What: Editing photos
When: Before sharing or printing
Where: On computer or phone apps
Why: Enhance quality or aesthetics
How: Using software or mobile apps

Answer: From time to time, yes. Sometimes, all a photo needs is a little touch-up to make it pop. As the saying goes, there's no harm in painting the lily a bit.

8. Have any photographs ever brought a tear to your eye or made you laugh out loud?

5W1H Ideas:
Who: I
What: Emotional response to photos
When: Upon viewing certain memorable photos
Where: At home or in exhibitions
Why: Due to the emotional content or memories
How: Instantly or after reminiscing

Answer: Oh, absolutely! Pictures have a way of freezing moments, and sometimes, just looking at an old photo can open the floodgates of emotions. They truly are a trip down memory lane.

PUBLIC TRANSPORT

1. How often do you use public transportation?

5W1H Ideas:
Who: I
What: Using public transportation
When: Daily/Weekly/Monthly
Where: Within the city or intercity
Why: To commute or travel
How: By bus, train, etc.

Answer: I use public transportation almost daily. It's the backbone of my commute, ensuring I get to places efficiently without the hassle of driving.

2. What's your preferred mode of public transport?

5W1H Ideas:
Who: I
What: Preferred mode
When: Depending on convenience or schedule
Where: Over different terrains or city routes
Why: Comfort, speed, or cost-effectiveness
How: Choosing based on experience

Answer: I have a soft spot for trains. They're not only spacious and comfortable but also often right on the dot, ensuring punctuality.

3. Do you think public transport is more economical than owning a car?

5W1H Ideas:
Who: I
What: Comparing costs of public transport and personal car
When: Considering daily commuting expenses
Where: Urban areas or any city
Why: Evaluating cost-efficiency
How: By comparing expenses, maintenance, and fuel costs

Answer: In the long run, I believe public transport often comes out on top in terms of cost. Owning a car has its perks, but when you factor in maintenance, fuel, and parking, it can burn a hole in your pocket.

4. Are public transport facilities in your area reliable?

5W1H Ideas:
Who: I
What: Reliability of public transport
When: Throughout the year
Where: In my locality or city
Why: Assessing dependability
How: Based on personal experience

Answer: By and large, they're quite reliable. There might be the occasional hiccup during peak hours or bad weather, but it's mostly smooth sailing.

5. How do you pass the time when you're on public transportation?

5W1H Ideas:
Who: I
What: Passing time
When: While on public transportation
Where: On buses, trains, etc.
Why: To keep entertained or be productive
How: Various activities

Answer: I usually have my nose buried in a book. It's a great way to make the journey fly by.

6. How do you feel about the cleanliness of public transport in your city?

5W1H Ideas:
Who: I
What: Feelings about cleanliness
When: Every time I use it
Where: In the city
Why: Personal comfort and hygiene
How: Observing and comparing

Answer: To be honest, it's hit or miss. Some vehicles are spotless, while others leave a lot to be desired.

7. Have you ever forgotten something on public transport?

5W1H Ideas:
Who: I
What: Forgetting an item
When: In the past
Where: On a bus, train, etc.
Why: Distraction or haste
How: Misplacing or oversight

Answer: Once or twice, I've had a memory lapse and left my umbrella or hat behind. It's easy to do when you're in a rush.

8. Do you prefer traveling by bus or train?

5W1H Ideas:
Who: I
What: Travel preference
When: Whenever needed
Where: Around the city or to other places
Why: Comfort or convenience
How: Personal choice based on experience

Answer: I'm more inclined towards trains. They often have fewer stops and offer a smoother ride.

9. Is public transport crowded during peak hours in your area?

5W1H Ideas:
Who: I
What: Crowdedness
When: Peak hours
Where: In the city or area
Why: Office or school timings
How: Based on observation

Answer: Absolutely. During rush hour, buses and trains are packed like sardines. It's a real test of patience.

10. Do you feel safe using public transport late at night?

5W1H Ideas:
Who: I
What: Feelings about safety
When: Late at night
Where: In the city or region
Why: Personal security concerns
How: Based on personal experiences or stories heard

Answer: Generally, I do. But it's always better to be safe than sorry, so I'm extra cautious and alert during those hours.

RECYCLING AND SUSTAINABILITY

1. Do you often recycle items at home?

5W1H Ideas:
Who: I
What: Recycling items
When: Regularly
Where: At home
Why: Environmental consciousness
How: Separating waste and using recycling bins

Answer: Yes, I make it a point to recycle items at home regularly. It's my little way of giving back to Mother Earth. By separating waste and using dedicated bins, I aim to reduce our household's environmental impact.

2. How do you feel about the importance of sustainability?

5W1H Ideas:
Who: I
What: Feelings about sustainability
When: Nowadays
Where: Globally
Why: Future generations' welfare
How: By practicing and promoting sustainable activities

Answer: Nowadays, I strongly believe that sustainability is the need of the hour. For the sake of our planet and future generations, we all must pitch in. By adopting sustainable practices in our daily lives, we can make a world of difference.

3. Are there recycling facilities near your residence?

5W1H Ideas:
Who: I
What: Recycling facilities
When: Currently
Where: Near my residence
Why: To promote recycling
How: Establishing dedicated centers

Answer: Yes, currently there are a few recycling facilities near where I live. These centers are set up to promote the culture of recycling and make it easier for residents like me to play our part.

4. Do you think recycling is a drop in the ocean when it comes to sustainability?

5W1H Ideas:
Who: I
What: Thoughts on recycling's impact
When: In the grand scheme of things
Where: In terms of global sustainability
Why: Due to the enormity of environmental issues
How: By comparing recycling to other sustainable practices

Answer: While some argue that recycling is just a drop in the ocean, I believe every bit counts. In the grand scheme, it's one of the many steps towards global sustainability. It's essential to understand the bigger picture and value each sustainable action.

5. How often do you use products made from recycled materials?

5W1H Ideas:
Who: I
What: Using recycled products
When: Whenever possible
Where: During shopping or daily use
Why: To support the recycling industry
How: By choosing them over non-recycled products

Answer: Whenever possible, I choose products made from recycled materials. It's my way of supporting the recycling industry and making sustainable choices during my shopping trips.

6. What do you think is the biggest hurdle to widespread recycling?

5W1H Ideas:
Who: I
What: Opinion on challenges
When: In current times
Where: Globally
Why: Due to lack of awareness or facilities
How: Observing global trends and reading up on issues

Answer: In my view, the biggest hurdle to widespread recycling nowadays is the lack of awareness and adequate facilities. If people are educated and given the right tools, they'd jump on the bandwagon in no time.

7. Do you think people have become more environmentally conscious over the years?

5W1H Ideas:
Who: People
What: Becoming environmentally conscious
When: Over the years
Where: Globally
Why: Due to increasing awareness and environmental challenges
How: Through campaigns, education, and media

Answer: Definitely, over the years, people worldwide seem to have woken up and smelled the coffee. There's a noticeable shift towards environmental consciousness, thanks to numerous campaigns and the alarming state of our planet.

8. Are there any sustainable products or practices you swear by?

5W1H Ideas:
Who: I
What: Sustainable products/practices
When: In my daily life
Where: At home or outside
Why: To reduce carbon footprint
How: By consciously choosing and using them

Answer: Absolutely, in my daily life, I always carry a reusable water bottle. It's a small step, but I believe it's better than adding to the mountain of single-use plastics out there.

9. How do local communities around you promote sustainable living?

5W1H Ideas:
Who: Local communities
What: Promoting sustainable living
When: In recent years
Where: In my locality
Why: To ensure a greener future
How: Through workshops, campaigns, and communal projects

Answer: In recent years, I've seen local communities pulling out all the stops. They conduct workshops and campaigns, focusing on everything from waste management to sustainable farming. It's heartening to witness.

10. Do you find it challenging to keep up with the three R's: Reduce, Reuse, and Recycle?

5W1H Ideas:
Who: I
What: Keeping up with the three R's
When: In my day-to-day life
Where: At home, work, or when shopping
Why: To maintain a sustainable lifestyle
How: By being mindful and practicing the principles

Answer: It can be a tightrope walk at times, balancing between convenience and sustainability. But I genuinely try to implement the three R's in my day-to-day life, especially when it comes to shopping and waste management.

ROLE MODELS AND INFLUENCES

1. Who is your role model?

5W1H Ideas:
Who: My favorite author
What: Being my role model
When: Since I started reading books
Where: In my personal growth journey
Why: Because of their wisdom and perspective
How: Through their writings and teachings

Answer: My favorite author, Bhai Vir Singh Ji, has been a guiding star for me since I delved into books. Their wisdom and unique perspective on life have profoundly influenced my personal growth.

2. Do you think celebrities make good role models?

5W1H Ideas:
Who: Celebrities
What: Being role models
When: In contemporary times
Where: In the media and public eye
Why: Because of their fame and influence
How: Through their actions and decisions

Answer: It's a mixed bag, really. Some celebrities truly shine bright, using their fame to inspire and bring about change. However, others might lead with questionable choices.

3. How have role models in society changed over time?

5W1H Ideas:
Who: Role models in society
What: Their evolution and change
When: Over the decades
Where: Globally
Why: Due to shifting values and cultural shifts
How: As a reflection of changing societal norms

Answer: It's like comparing apples and oranges. Role models from decades ago embodied different values, often aligned with societal norms of their times. Nowadays, there's a broader spectrum, reflecting our diverse, global world.

4. Can fictional characters be considered role models?

5W1H Ideas:
Who: Fictional characters
What: Being viewed as role models
When: While consuming media (books, movies)
Where: In literature and entertainment
Why: Because of their impactful stories and characteristics
How: Through their actions, decisions, and growth in stories

Answer: Absolutely, fictional characters can sometimes leave an indelible mark on our minds. Their stories, actions, or resilience can inspire us in real life, making us believe that every cloud has a silver lining.

5. Who was your role model when you were a child?

5W1H Ideas:
Who: My grandfather
What: My childhood role model
When: During my early years
Where: At our family home
Why: Due to his wisdom and kindness
How: Through his daily actions and stories

Answer: Growing up, my grandfather was someone I looked up to. His kindness and the tales of his experiences always resonated with me.

6. Are there any athletes you admire?

5W1H Ideas:
Who: Famous hockey player
What: Being admired
When: Since I started watching tennis
Where: On the football court and in interviews
Why: Because of their dedication and skill
How: By watching their matches and following their career

Answer: I've always been a big fan of soccer, and there's one player whose dedication and prowess on the court really stands out to me. His name is Major Dhyan Chand.

7. Do you have any teachers who have influenced you?

5W1H Ideas:
Who: My history teacher
What: Influencing my love for history
When: During high school
Where: In the classroom
Why: Through engaging lessons and personal anecdotes
How: By making the subject come alive

Answer: Back in high school, my history teacher had a knack for bringing the past to life, which sparked my passion for the subject.

8. Have you ever looked up to a fictional hero?

5W1H Ideas:
Who: A superhero from a famous movie
What: Being an inspiration
When: After watching the film
Where: In the cinema and later in discussions
Why: Because of their values and actions
How: Through the plot and character development

Answer: After watching a certain superhero movie, Batman- Dark Knight, I was really taken by the lead character's values and actions.

9. Do you believe parents should be role models for their kids?

5W1H Ideas:
Who: Parents
What: Acting as role models
When: Throughout a child's life
Where: At home and in public
Why: To guide and teach their children
How: Through their actions, decisions, and behaviors

Answer: Without a doubt, parents play a pivotal role in shaping their kids, so it's crucial for them to set a good example at all times.

10. Is there a historical figure you greatly respect?

5W1H Ideas:
Who: A famous leader from the past
What: Gaining respect
When: After reading about them in school
Where: In history books
Why: Because of their contributions and leadership
How: By their impact on society and the world

Answer: I remember reading about a certain historical leader, Subash Chandra Bose, in school, and his contributions to society left a lasting impression on me

SEA AND OCEANS

1. Do you like visiting the beach?

5W1H Ideas:
Who: I
What: Enjoying beach visits
When: Whenever I get a chance
Where: Local beaches and during vacations
Why: Love for the sea and relaxation
How: By spending hours lounging and playing

Answer: I absolutely adore visiting the beach. Whenever there's an opportunity, whether it's close by or during my vacations, I'm there. The sound of the waves is so relaxing, and I can spend hours just lounging on the sand and playing in the water. For me, the beach is where I feel as free as a bird.

2. Have you ever tried water sports?

5W1H Ideas:
Who: I
What: Trying water sports
When: Last summer
Where: At a coastal resort
Why: Adventure and thrill-seeking
How: By renting equipment and taking a quick lesson

Answer: Indeed, last summer I dived right into water sports during my stay at a coastal resort. I've always had this itch for adventure, so I rented some equipment and even took a quick lesson. The experience was a whole new ball game for me and filled with thrill.

3. Do you think oceans are important for our planet?

5W1H Ideas:
Who: We, as humans
What: Recognizing the importance of oceans
When: Always
Where: Globally
Why: Oceans regulate climate, support biodiversity, and more
How: Through their vastness and richness

Answer: Absolutely, oceans are undeniably crucial for our Earth. Always and everywhere, they play a pivotal role. From regulating our climate to supporting a myriad of biodiversity, the vastness and richness of oceans are simply unparalleled. To put it another way, they are the lifeblood of our planet.

4. Are you concerned about sea pollution?

5W1H Ideas:
Who: I and many others
What: Concerns about sea pollution
When: In recent years
Where: All over the world
Why: Increasing waste and its impact on marine life
How: Through news, reports, and personal observations

Answer: In recent years, my concern, shared by many others, about sea pollution has amplified. No matter where in the world you go, it's evident. The alarming rise in waste and its devastating impact on marine life is deeply troubling. Through news and personal observations, it's clear as day that we're facing a pressing challenge.

5. Have you ever been on a boat or ship?

5W1H Ideas:
Who: I
What: Traveling on a boat/ship
When: A couple of years ago
Where: During a coastal vacation
Why: For sightseeing and the experience
How: By booking a tour

Answer: Yes, a couple of years ago, I embarked on a journey by boat. It was during a coastal vacation, and the main draw for me was the unique sightseeing opportunities and the sheer joy of the experience. After booking a local tour, I set sail, and I must say, the entire trip was smooth sailing with breathtaking views.

6. Do you enjoy seafood?

5W1H Ideas:
Who: I
What: Relishing seafood
When: Every now and then
Where: At seafood restaurants
Why: Due to its rich flavors and health benefits
How: Grilled, fried, or in a curry

Answer: Oh, hook, line, and sinker, I'm a massive fan of seafood! Every so often, you'll find me at seafood restaurants, savoring the rich flavors. Whether it's grilled, fried, or in a delightful curry, I simply can't resist. It's not just the taste; the health benefits of seafood are a cherry on top.

7. Have you ever tried deep-sea diving?

5W1H Ideas:
Who: I
What: Attempting deep-sea diving
When: During a trip last year
Where: A coral reef in the Maldives
Why: Fascination with underwater world
How: With a certified instructor and diving gear

Answer: Last year, I took the plunge and tried deep-sea diving in the Maldives, right around a vibrant coral reef. My fascination with the underwater world made me eager to explore its depths. I wasn't swimming solo, though; a certified instructor was my guide, ensuring I was equipped with the right gear. It was a deep dive into another realm, and to say I was over the moon would be an understatement.

8. Do you prefer the sea's calmness or its raging waves?

5W1H Ideas:
Who: I
What: Preference between sea's calmness and raging waves
When: Depending on mood and occasion
Where: Beaches and coastlines
Why: Different experiences and emotions
How: Observing or being in the water

Answer: At different times, I've felt drawn to both the sea's serenity and its wild waves. The tranquil shores are perfect when I want to reflect or just get lost in thoughts, while the roaring waves stir up excitement, almost like nature's own roller coaster. As the saying goes, 'life's a beach,' and the sea's moods certainly add to its allure.

SHOPPING AND GIFTS

1. How often do you go shopping for clothes?

5W1H Ideas:
Who: I
What: Shopping for clothes
When: Every few months
Where: Local mall or online
Why: Update wardrobe or for special occasions
How: Browse, try on, and then buy

Answer: Every few months, I find myself heading to the local mall or checking online stores to update my wardrobe. Sometimes, it's for special occasions, but mostly just to freshen up my style. As they say, clothes make the man, and I do feel good in something new!

2. Do you prefer buying gifts or receiving them?

5W1H Ideas:
Who: I
What: Buying gifts vs. receiving them
When: On special occasions
Where: From various stores or online
Why: Joy of giving or the surprise of receiving
How: Thoughtfully selecting or graciously accepting

Answer: I cherish the joy of giving. There's something truly special about thoughtfully selecting a gift for someone and then watching their reaction. As the idiom goes, 'it's the thought that counts,' and I wholeheartedly believe in it!

3. Are there any traditional gifts in your culture?

5W1H Ideas:
Who: People in my culture
What: Traditional gifts
When: During cultural festivities or occasions
Where: In my country
Why: Celebrate and uphold traditions
How: Handcrafted items, special artifacts

Answer: In our culture, we have a tradition of giving handcrafted items or special artifacts during particular festivities. These traditional gifts are not just tokens but carry a deeper meaning, representing our heritage. It's a 'blast from the past' in a beautiful, tangible form.

4. Do you like window shopping?

5W1H Ideas:
Who: I
What: Window shopping
When: Occasionally, during weekends
Where: At the high street or shopping centers
Why: Leisure, or to get an idea of what's trending
How: Strolling and observing without buying

Answer: Occasionally, I do indulge in window shopping, especially during weekends. It's more of a leisure activity for me, allowing me to see what's trending without actually buying. It's a great way to 'kill two birds with one stone' – getting some walking in while also checking out the latest fashions.

5. Are you a fan of online shopping?

5W1H Ideas:
Who: I
What: Online shopping
When: When deals are attractive or for convenience
Where: Various e-commerce websites
Why: Convenience or attractive deals
How: Browsing, adding to cart, and ordering

Answer: Absolutely, I often find myself surfing e-commerce websites for the sheer convenience they offer. Sometimes it's the attractive deals that pull me in. Being able to shop without leaving my couch feels like having 'the best of both worlds.'

6. Have you ever given a handmade gift?

5W1H Ideas:
Who: I
What: Giving a handmade gift
When: On a dear friend's birthday
Where: At a friend's place
Why: Personal touch and significance
How: Crafted with care and given with love

Answer: Yes, I once crafted a handmade gift for a dear friend's birthday. I believe that such gifts carry a personal touch and signify the time and effort invested. As they say, 'actions speak louder than words,' and a handmade gift speaks volumes about one's feelings.

7. What was the last gift you purchased?

5W1H Ideas:
Who: I
What: Last gift purchased
When: Last month
Where: At a boutique store
Why: For my sister's graduation
How: After careful consideration and selection

Answer: Last month, I picked up a beautiful necklace from a boutique store as a gift for my sister's graduation. I wanted to give her something memorable, and this seemed perfect. You know, 'a thing of beauty is a joy forever,' and I believe she'll cherish it.

8. Do you think gifts should always be expensive?

5W1H Ideas:
Who: People in general
What: Perception of gifts' value
When: While giving or receiving gifts
Where: Anywhere gifts are exchanged
Why: To show appreciation or affection
How: Through thought, effort, and the meaning behind them

Answer: I don't believe that the value of a gift lies in its price tag. Often, it's the thought, effort, and the sentiment behind it that matter most. As the saying goes, 'it's the thought that counts,' and truly heartfelt gifts are beyond any price.

SOCIAL MEDIA AND THE INTERNET

1. How often do you check your social media accounts?

5W1H Ideas:
Who: I
What: Check social media accounts
When: Several times a day
Where: Usually on my phone
Why: To stay updated
How: Quick scrolls or deep dives depending on time

Answer: Several times a day, I'm on my phone, scrolling through my social media feeds. It's just a way for me to stay updated, sometimes quickly, sometimes I dive in deeper. As they say, 'keeping up with the times.'

2. Which social media platform do you prefer?

5W1H Ideas:
Who: I
What: Preferred social media platform
When: Daily usage
Where: On various devices
Why: To connect, share, and explore
How: Browsing and interacting

Answer: I'm quite keen on Instagram. Daily, on various devices, I use it to connect, share, and explore. It's a 'window to the world' in many ways, letting me interact in dynamic ways.

3. Have you ever taken a break from social media?

5W1H Ideas:
Who: I
What: Break from social media
When: Occasionally, for detox
Where: Offline, engaging in other activities
Why: Mental well-being
How: By deliberately logging off and focusing elsewhere

Answer: Occasionally, for my mental well-being, I deliberately log off and engage in other offline activities. It's my way of 'recharging my batteries' and ensuring I don't get too absorbed.

4. How has the internet influenced your daily life?

5W1H Ideas:
Who: I
What: Influence of the internet
When: Daily, for various tasks
Where: At home, work, on the go
Why: Information, connectivity, entertainment
How: Accessing, researching, communicating

Answer: The internet has woven its way into almost every facet of my daily life. Be it at home, work, or on the go, I rely on it for information, connectivity, and entertainment. It's like having a 'world at my fingertips.'

5. Do you think we share too much online?

5W1H Ideas:
Who: People in general
What: Sharing online
When: Frequently
Where: On social platforms
Why: Express, update, or for validation
How: Posting, commenting, reacting

Answer: People, in general, seem to share quite frequently on online platforms, be it to express, update or sometimes even for validation. Sometimes, it feels like 'too much information,' but it varies from person to person.

6. How do you ensure your safety on the internet?

5W1H Ideas:
Who: I
What: Ensuring safety
When: Whenever online
Where: Across various websites and platforms
Why: To protect personal information
How: Using strong passwords, avoiding suspicious links

Answer: Whenever I'm online, safety is paramount. Across all platforms, I ensure to use strong passwords and always remain wary of suspicious links. It's always better to be 'safe than sorry.'

7. Do you follow any influencers or bloggers on social media?

5W1H Ideas:
Who: I
What: Following influencers or bloggers
When: As they post updates
Where: On platforms like Instagram, YouTube, etc.
Why: For inspiration, entertainment, or information
How: Subscribing, liking, and engaging

Answer: Yes, I do follow a few influencers on platforms like Instagram. They offer a good mix of inspiration, entertainment, and sometimes valuable information. It's like 'catching a glimpse' into various lifestyles and perspectives.

8. What's your take on online friendships?

5W1H Ideas:
Who: I
What: Perspective on online friendships
When: In the age of digital connectivity
Where: Over the internet
Why: Expanding social circles or shared interests
How: Engaging, chatting, and building trust

Answer: In today's digital age, I believe online friendships can be as genuine as offline ones. Over the internet, we can engage, chat, and bond over shared interests. It's a way to 'expand horizons' socially without geographical constraints.

SPACE AND ASTRONOMY

1. How often do you stargaze at night?

5W1H Ideas:
Who: I
What: Stargaze
When: Occasionally on clear nights
Where: From my balcony or a park
Why: To relax and marvel at the universe
How: Just with my eyes or using a telescope

Answer: On clear nights, I occasionally stargaze from my balcony. It's a way for me to 'lose myself' in the vastness of the universe, either just with my eyes or sometimes using a telescope.

2. Do you have a favorite planet?

5W1H Ideas:
Who: I
What: Favorite planet
When: Since studying it in school
Where: In our solar system
Why: Because of its unique features
How: By reading and watching documentaries

Answer: Ever since school, I've been fascinated by Saturn, especially in our solar system. Its rings and unique features 'stand out from the crowd.' I've learned a lot about it through books and documentaries.

3. Would you like to travel to space someday?

5W1H Ideas:
Who: I
What: Space travel
When: In the future, if possible
Where: Maybe to the Moon or Mars
Why: To experience the unknown
How: On a space mission or commercial space flight

Answer: If given the chance in the future, I'd love to embark on a journey to space, perhaps to the Moon or Mars. The idea of experiencing the unknown is 'out of this world' and it'd be a dream come true.

4. How do you keep updated with space news?

5W1H Ideas:
Who: I
What: Keeping updated with space news
When: Regularly
Where: Online websites and science magazines
Why: Curiosity and interest in the universe
How: Reading articles and watching videos

Answer: I regularly 'dive deep' into the world of online websites and science magazines to keep myself updated with space news. My curiosity about the universe drives me to read articles and watch insightful videos.

5. Do you believe in extraterrestrial life?

5W1H Ideas:
Who: I
What: Belief in extraterrestrial life
When: Given the vastness of the universe
Where: Possibly in other galaxies or planets
Why: Universe's vastness and potential
How: Based on scientific hypotheses and personal belief

Answer: Given the sheer vastness of the universe, I do entertain the thought of extraterrestrial life. The idea that we might not be alone is 'food for thought,' and science keeps bringing up intriguing possibilities.

6. Have you visited any planetariums or observatories?

5W1H Ideas:
Who: I
What: Visited planetariums or observatories
When: A few times in the past
Where: During school trips or vacations
Why: To learn and experience astronomy firsthand
How: By attending shows or observing celestial objects

Answer: A few times, especially during school trips or vacations, I've visited planetariums and observatories. They offer a 'window to the stars,' allowing me to learn and experience the wonders of astronomy firsthand.

7. How do you feel about space exploration?

5W1H Ideas:
Who: I
What: Feelings about space exploration
When: Considering recent advancements
Where: Beyond Earth, to other planets and galaxies
Why: To understand the universe and our place in it
How: By supporting space agencies and missions

Answer: Considering the recent advancements, I feel quite optimistic about space exploration. Venturing beyond Earth, understanding our universe, and finding our place in it is 'a giant leap for mankind'. I wholeheartedly support such missions.

8. Do you enjoy watching documentaries about space?

5W1H Ideas:
Who: I
What: Enjoyment of space documentaries
When: In my free time
Where: On TV or streaming platforms
Why: Intrigue and thirst for knowledge
How: By choosing popular or recommended series

Answer: In my leisure, I absolutely 'get lost in' documentaries about space on TV or streaming platforms. The intrigue and thirst for knowledge about our universe never cease to amaze me.

SPORTS AND PHYSICAL ACTIVITIES

1. How often do you play sports or engage in physical activities?

5W1H Ideas:
Who: I
What: Play sports or engage in physical activities
When: Almost every weekend
Where: At a nearby sports center or park
Why: To stay fit and refresh my mind
How: By playing badminton or jogging

Answer: Almost every weekend, I 'hit the ground running' at a nearby sports center or park. Whether it's playing badminton or just jogging, I do it to stay fit and rejuvenate my mind.

2. Do you have a favorite sport you like to watch or play?

5W1H Ideas:
Who: I
What: A favorite sport
When: Since my childhood
Where: On TV or at local stadiums
Why: I love the strategy and excitement it offers
How: By following matches and practicing occasionally

Answer: Since my younger days, I've been 'bowled over' by cricket. I often watch matches on TV or at local stadiums and occasionally practice. The strategy and thrill it offers are just unparalleled.

3. Are there any sports you'd like to try in the future?

5W1H Ideas:
Who: I
What: New sports to try
When: In the near future
Where: Perhaps in a specialized sports club
Why: To learn new skills and challenges
How: By taking beginner courses or lessons

Answer: In the near future, I have a 'burning desire' to try out archery. The thought of learning new skills and facing unique challenges excites me. I'm considering beginner courses at a sports club.

4. How do physical activities impact your mood and health?

5W1H Ideas:
Who: I
What: Impact of physical activities
When: After engaging in them
Where: Both mentally and physically
Why: They boost my energy and reduce stress
How: By releasing endorphins and promoting good health

Answer: After breaking a sweat, I always feel 'on top of the world.' Physical activities not only enhance my energy but significantly reduce stress. It's all about those endorphins and the holistic benefits they offer.

5. Did you play any sports in school?

5W1H Ideas:
Who: I
What: Played sports
When: During my school years
Where: In school competitions
Why: To represent my class and enjoy team spirit
How: By being part of the school's football team

Answer: During school, I was 'knee-deep' in football and represented my class in various competitions. Being a part of the team was exhilarating, and I thoroughly enjoyed the camaraderie.

6. Are there any fitness trends you've noticed becoming popular recently?

5W1H Ideas:
Who: I
What: Noticed fitness trends
When: In recent times
Where: Online and in fitness centers
Why: To adapt to new methods of staying fit
How: By following influencers and attending workshops

Answer: Of late, I've noticed that yoga and pilates are 'making waves' in the fitness scene. Many people, influenced by online personalities or workshops, are turning to these methods for a balanced fitness approach.

7. Do you prefer indoor or outdoor activities?

5W1H Ideas:
Who: I
What: Preference for activities
When: During my free time
Where: Either at home or outdoors
Why: Depends on the mood and weather
How: By choosing activities like reading indoors or hiking outdoors

Answer: My preferences 'swing both ways.' At times, I'm content with indoor activities like reading, but when the weather's inviting, nothing beats the allure of an outdoor hike.

8. How important is it for children to be involved in sports?

5W1H Ideas:
Who: Children
What: Involvement in sports
When: During their formative years
Where: At schools or community centers
Why: To develop physical and social skills
How: By participating in school teams or local clubs

Answer: It's 'of paramount importance' for children to dive into sports during their formative years. Beyond the obvious physical benefits, it molds their social skills and team spirit.

TECHNOLOGY AND GADGETS

1. How often do you use electronic gadgets in your daily life?

5W1H Ideas:
Who: I
What: Use electronic gadgets
When: Daily
Where: At home, work, and on the go
Why: To stay connected and be productive
How: Primarily through my smartphone and laptop

Answer: I 'plug into' the digital world daily, be it at home or work. My smartphone and laptop are my lifelines, helping me stay connected and enhancing my productivity.

2. Do you have a favorite piece of technology that you own?

5W1H Ideas:
Who: I
What: A favorite tech item
When: Currently
Where: Mostly at home
Why: Because of its utility and features
How: By using it for entertainment and work

Answer: My smart speaker has 'stolen the spotlight' at my home. I use it both for work reminders and unwinding with some music. It's a marvelous blend of utility and entertainment.

3. Are there any technological advancements you're excited about?

5W1H Ideas:
Who: I
What: Excited about tech advancements
When: In the near future
Where: In the tech industry
Why: Due to the potential positive changes they can bring
How: By following tech news and updates

Answer: I'm 'all ears' when it comes to augmented reality (AR) developments. The potential transformations AR can bring to the education and entertainment sectors are truly intriguing.

4. How has technology impacted your personal relationships?

5W1H Ideas:
Who: I and my personal relationships
What: Impact of technology
When: Over recent years
Where: In terms of communication
Why: Due to easier and instantaneous communication
How: By using apps and social media

Answer: Technology has 'bridged the gap' in my personal relationships. Apps and social platforms allow instant communication, making it easier to nurture bonds even from miles away.

5. Do you think you spend too much time on gadgets?

5W1H Ideas:
Who: I
What: Time spent on gadgets
When: Daily
Where: Especially at home
Why: Due to work and leisure activities
How: By browsing, working, and streaming

Answer: At times, I feel like I'm 'living in a digital bubble,' especially at home. The overlap of work and leisure activities on gadgets makes it hard to disconnect.

6. How do you ensure you take breaks from screen time?

5W1H Ideas:
Who: I
What: Ensure breaks from screens
When: Throughout the day
Where: At work and home
Why: For eye health and mental well-being
How: By setting alarms and indulging in non-tech activities

Answer: To 'switch gears' and reduce screen strain, I set periodic alarms reminding me to take a break. It's an opportunity to stretch or dive into a good old-fashioned book.

7. What's the most recent gadget you've purchased?

5W1H Ideas:
Who: I
What: The most recent tech purchase
When: Last month
Where: From an online store
Why: To enhance my work efficiency
How: After researching the best models

Answer: Last month, I 'bit the bullet' and bought a tablet from an online store. It's a game-changer for my work efficiency, especially after doing extensive research on the best models.

8. How do you feel about the increasing reliance on technology?

5W1H Ideas:
Who: Society and I
What: Feelings on increasing tech reliance
When: In this modern era
Where: Globally
Why: It's a double-edged sword with benefits and pitfalls
How: By observing societal changes and personal experiences

Answer: In today's age, our growing reliance on technology feels like a 'double-edged sword.' While it offers unparalleled convenience, there's a looming fear of becoming too dependent.

TELEVISION AND MOVIES

1. How often do you watch movies or television shows?

5W1H Ideas:
Who: I
What: Watch movies and TV shows
When: Mostly during weekends
Where: At home on my couch
Why: For relaxation and entertainment
How: Through streaming platforms

Answer: I usually 'tune in' to movies and TV shows on weekends, lounging on my couch at home. Streaming platforms have become my go-to for relaxation and entertainment.

2. Do you have a favorite film genre?

5W1H Ideas:
Who: I
What: Favorite film genre
When: Always
Where: In cinemas or at home
Why: It resonates with my interests
How: By repeatedly choosing it over others

Answer: I've always been 'drawn like a moth to a flame' to mystery films. Whether at the cinema or home, the suspense and unpredictability keep me hooked.

3. How do movies from your country differ from Hollywood productions?

5W1H Ideas:
Who: Movies from my country and Hollywood
What: Differences in production
When: Historically and currently
Where: In themes, budget, and style
Why: Due to cultural nuances and budgeting
How: By portraying local narratives and customs

Answer: Movies from my country 'paint a different picture' compared to Hollywood. They often dive deep into local narratives, customs, and sometimes operate on tighter budgets.

4. Do you prefer watching movies at home or in a cinema?

5W1H Ideas:
Who: I
What: Preference in watching movies
When: Whenever a good movie releases
Where: At home or in cinema
Why: For comfort or the cinematic experience
How: Alone or with friends

Answer: While home offers comfort, there's something 'larger than life' about the cinema experience. So, whenever a blockbuster releases, I prefer the cinema's immersive feel.

5. How have TV shows evolved in your country over the past decade?

5W1H Ideas:
Who: TV shows in my country
What: Evolution over time
When: Over the past decade
Where: In terms of themes, quality, and presentation
Why: Influence of globalization and changing viewer preferences
How: By incorporating modern narratives and higher production values

Answer: TV shows in my country have 'come a long way' in the past decade. Modern narratives, higher production values, and a touch of global influences have reshaped our television landscape.

6. Do you think movies and TV shows influence societal behavior?

5W1H Ideas:
Who: Movies and TV shows
What: Influence on society
When: Throughout history and now
Where: In terms of trends, norms, and values
Why: They reflect and shape culture
How: By portraying certain behaviors and ideals

Answer: Movies and TV shows undoubtedly 'hold a mirror' to society. They not only reflect cultural norms but also have the power to shape trends and values over time.

7. How do you usually choose which movie or TV show to watch?

5W1H Ideas:
Who: I
What: Choosing movies or TV shows
When: During my leisure time
Where: At home or cinema
Why: Based on mood, reviews, or recommendations
How: By browsing streaming platforms or seeking suggestions

Answer: I 'go with the flow' when choosing movies. Depending on my mood, I'll browse through streaming platforms, or if a friend raves about something, I'll give it a shot.

8. Are there any actors or directors from your country who have made it big internationally?

5W1H Ideas:
Who: Actors or directors from my country
What: Achieving international fame
When: In recent years
Where: In international film festivals or Hollywood
Why: Due to their talent and unique perspective
How: By working in acclaimed international projects

Answer: Yes, a few talents from my country have 'made waves' internationally, especially in film festivals and even Hollywood. Their unique perspectives and undeniable skills have paved the way.

TIME MANAGEMENT

1. How do you usually plan your day?

5W1H Ideas:
Who: I
What: Plan my day
When: Every morning
Where: At home, using a planner or digital tools
Why: To be organized and efficient
How: By setting priorities and allocating time slots

Answer: Every morning, I 'take the bull by the horns' and plan my day using a digital tool. Setting priorities helps me stay organized and make the most of my time.

2. Do you think having a routine is beneficial?

5W1H Ideas:
Who: I, and most people
What: Opinion on having a routine
When: Daily
Where: In personal and professional life
Why: For consistency and discipline
How: By following a set pattern

Answer: I truly believe that 'old habits die hard', and having a routine ingrains consistency and discipline in one's life, which can be pivotal for achieving long-term goals.

3. How do you prioritize tasks when you're short on time?

5W1H Ideas:
Who: I
What: Prioritizing tasks
When: When running against the clock
Where: At work or home
Why: To ensure essential tasks get completed
How: By assessing urgency and importance

Answer: When I'm 'pressed for time', I weigh tasks based on their urgency and importance. This ensures that I tackle the essential things first and push less crucial tasks for later.

4. Do you often use any tools or apps to manage your time?

5W1H Ideas:
Who: I
What: Using tools/apps for time management
When: Daily or frequently
Where: On my computer or phone
Why: To streamline activities and reminders
How: By setting tasks, reminders, and events

Answer: Yes, I 'keep up with the times' by using digital tools and apps on my phone to manage my tasks and set reminders. They help streamline my activities and ensure I don't forget anything.

5. How do you handle interruptions when you're focused on a task?

5W1H Ideas:
Who: I
What: Handling interruptions
When: While deep in work
Where: At work or during personal projects
Why: To maintain productivity
How: By setting boundaries or using strategies like the Pomodoro Technique

Answer: When I'm 'in the zone', I try to fend off interruptions by setting clear boundaries. If something unexpected pops up, I use techniques like the Pomodoro to ensure I return to my task promptly.

6. Are there any time management techniques you swear by?

5W1H Ideas:
Who: I
What: Time management techniques
When: When handling multiple tasks
Where: At work or during personal endeavors
Why: To increase efficiency
How: By employing specific strategies

Answer: Absolutely, I 'put all my eggs in one basket' with the Eisenhower Box method. It helps me classify tasks based on their urgency and importance, making my day more productive.

7. How do you ensure you have some leisure time daily?

5W1H Ideas:
Who: I
What: Ensuring leisure time
When: Every day
Where: At home or outdoors
Why: To relax and recharge
How: By deliberately blocking time slots

Answer: I believe 'all work and no play makes Jack a dull boy'. So, I consciously block out time slots daily, ensuring I get moments to unwind, whether at home or outdoors.

8. Do you often feel overwhelmed with too many tasks?

5W1H Ideas:
Who: I
What: Feelings regarding numerous tasks
When: Occasionally, especially during busy days
Where: At work or personal projects
Why: Due to accumulating responsibilities
How: By trying to multitask or pushing through

Answer: Every once in a while, when tasks 'pile up', I feel a bit overwhelmed. But I've learned that taking a step back, re-evaluating, and then diving back in helps regain clarity.

TRADITIONAL CRAFTS

1. Are there any traditional crafts popular in your country?

5W1H Ideas:
Who: Locals in my country
What: Traditional crafts
When: Historically and even now
Where: Across various regions in my country
Why: Cultural heritage and identity
How: Through traditional methods passed down generations

Answer: Yes, in my country, traditional crafts are the 'heart and soul' of our cultural heritage. Passed down generations, they reflect our identity and are popular across various regions.

2. Did you ever try your hand at any craft as a child?

5W1H Ideas:
Who: I, as a child
What: Trying out crafts
When: During school or summer vacations
Where: At home or school
Why: For fun and learning
How: With the help of craft kits or under guidance

Answer: As a child, I 'dipped my toes' into crafting during school projects or summer breaks. It was a blend of fun and learning, often using craft kits or under someone's guidance.

3. How important is it to preserve traditional crafts?

5W1H Ideas:
Who: Society and younger generations
What: Preserving traditional crafts
When: Continuously
Where: Globally, especially in places with rich heritage
Why: To protect cultural identity
How: Through education, workshops, and support

Answer: It's 'of paramount importance' to preserve traditional crafts. They're the cornerstone of our cultural identity, and continuous efforts through education and workshops are crucial.

4. Are handmade crafts expensive in your country?

5W1H Ideas:
Who: Craftsmen and buyers
What: Selling and buying handmade crafts
When: Presently
Where: In markets and craft fairs
Why: Due to manual effort and uniqueness
How: By pricing based on effort, material, and skill

Answer: In my country, handmade crafts often 'cost an arm and a leg' primarily because of the manual effort and uniqueness each piece brings. The pricing usually reflects the craftsmanship.

5. Do schools in your country teach traditional crafts?

5W1H Ideas:
Who: Schools and students
What: Teaching traditional crafts
When: During art and craft classes
Where: In educational institutions
Why: To impart cultural knowledge
How: Through special craft lessons or workshops

Answer: Yes, schools in my country 'go the extra mile' to impart our cultural heritage by including traditional crafts in the curriculum, usually through special workshops or art classes.

6. Do tourists buy these crafts as souvenirs?

5W1H Ideas:
Who: Tourists
What: Buying traditional crafts
When: During their visits
Where: From local markets or craft fairs
Why: As mementos or gifts
How: Based on attraction, quality, and affordability

Answer: Absolutely! Tourists 'flock like bees to honey' when it comes to our traditional crafts. They often purchase them from local markets as souvenirs or gifts to take back home.

7. Are young people interested in traditional crafts nowadays?

5W1H Ideas:
Who: Young people
What: Interest in traditional crafts
When: In contemporary times
Where: Urban and rural areas
Why: To connect with roots or for hobbies
How: By learning from elders or workshops

Answer: While 'old is gold', the interest in traditional crafts among young people is a mixed bag. Some are keen to connect with their roots, while others lean towards modern hobbies.

8. Do you own any items made through traditional craftsmanship?

5W1H Ideas:
Who: I
What: Owning traditional craft items
When: Purchased over the years
Where: From markets, fairs, or inherited
Why: Appreciation and utility
How: Bought or received as gifts

Answer: Yes, I have a few items that 'stand the test of time', crafted traditionally. I've bought some from markets, while others are gifts or inherited heirlooms.

TRAVEL AND HOLIDAYS

1. How often do you travel for leisure?

5W1H Ideas:
Who: I
What: Traveling for leisure
When: Depending on work and holidays
Where: Local getaways or abroad
Why: To relax and explore new places
How: By planning trips during vacations

Answer: I 'hit the road' for leisure maybe once or twice a year, depending on my work schedule. It's a way for me to relax and satiate my wanderlust.

2. Do you prefer beach holidays or mountain getaways?

5W1H Ideas:
Who: I
What: Beach holidays vs. mountain getaways
When: During vacation planning
Where: Coastal areas or hilly regions
Why: Personal preference and mood
How: Based on experiences and holiday objectives

Answer: I'm 'caught between a rock and a hard place' when choosing. Sometimes I crave the serenity of mountains, and other times I yearn for beach vibes.

3. What do you usually pack when going on vacation?

5W1H Ideas:
Who: I
What: Packing essentials for vacation
When: Before my travel date
Where: At my home
Why: To be prepared for the trip
How: Depending on the destination and duration

Answer: When packing, I always 'play it safe'. I pack according to the destination's weather, ensuring essentials like clothes, toiletries, and my camera are included.

4. Do you enjoy traveling solo or with a group?

5W1H Ideas:
Who: I
What: Traveling solo vs. group travel
When: During each travel opportunity
Where: Various destinations
Why: Based on comfort and the nature of the trip
How: By assessing my mood and trip objectives

Answer: While there's a 'method to my madness', I generally lean towards group travel. It offers companionship, but sometimes solo trips give me the peace I seek.

5. Is there a holiday that you fondly remember?

5W1H Ideas:
Who: I
What: A memorable holiday
When: In the past
Where: A particular destination
Why: Due to experiences or company
How: By cherishing memories

Answer: Yes, a trip to Bali 'takes the cake'. The blend of culture, nature, and the sea, combined with the company of good friends, made it unforgettable.

6. How do you usually plan your holidays?

5W1H Ideas:
Who: I
What: Planning holidays
When: Before the actual travel
Where: At home or with friends
Why: To ensure a smooth trip
How: By researching and making bookings

Answer: I typically 'leave no stone unturned' when planning holidays. I research extensively, consult friends, and book in advance to ensure a hassle-free experience.

7. Are there any travel destinations on your bucket list?

5W1H Ideas:
Who: I
What: Travel destinations to visit
When: In the future
Where: Global locations
Why: Dreams and aspirations
How: By saving and planning

Answer: Oh, absolutely! 'Rome wasn't built in a day', and likewise, it takes time to fulfill travel dreams. Places like New Zealand and Japan are high on my bucket list.

8. How do you feel about touristy spots vs. off-the-beaten-path locations?

5W1H Ideas:
Who: I
What: Preference between popular and lesser-known spots
When: While choosing destinations
Where: Around the world
Why: For unique experiences
How: Based on previous travels and advice

Answer: It's 'six of one, half a dozen of the other' for me. While touristy spots offer iconic experiences, off-the-beaten-path locations provide a sense of discovery and peace.

URBAN AND RURAL LIFE

1. Do you live in an urban or rural area?

5W1H Ideas:
Who: I
What: Living in an area
When: Currently
Where: Either urban or rural area
Why: Based on circumstances or personal choice
How: By residing and engaging with the community

Answer: Currently, I reside in an urban area, immersed in its pulsating energy and diverse opportunities. This setting aligns with my professional pursuits and social preferences, providing a dynamic environment that keeps me engaged and connected.

2. What do you like about living there?

5W1H Ideas:
Who: I
What: Liking aspects of the area
When: Presently
Where: In the current residence
Why: Due to positive and appealing features
How: By enjoying and appreciating the environment

Answer: I'm enamored with the urban lifestyle, where every day feels like a new adventure. The mosaic of cultures, the accessibility to amenities, and the endless career opportunities create an atmosphere that's both invigorating and inspiring.

3. What are some challenges of living in your area?

5W1H Ideas:
Who: I
What: Facing challenges
When: Occasionally
Where: In the urban area
Why: Due to the inherent issues of the location
How: By navigating through daily life

Answer: Living in the city isn't without its challenges; the fast-paced environment can be exhausting, and the cost of living is relatively high. Navigating through the hectic traffic and dealing with noise pollution are part of the daily grind, requiring adaptability and patience.

4. Is your neighborhood quiet or busy?

5W1H Ideas:
Who: I
What: Describing the neighborhood
When: Currently
Where: In my neighborhood
Why: To convey the environment
How: Based on daily observation

Answer: My neighborhood is a beehive of activity, constantly buzzing with people and vehicles. Though lively, sometimes the quietude of a serene countryside seems like a distant, tempting dream.

5. Are there many facilities near your home?

5W1H Ideas:
Who: I
What: Facilities availability
When: Currently
Where: Near my home
Why: For convenience
How: Through community planning

Answer: My vicinity boasts a plethora of facilities, making life not just convenient but vibrant. Everything is at arm's length, from recreational parks to shopping malls, embodying urban living's comfort and accessibility.

6. Would you prefer living in the countryside?

5W1H Ideas:
Who: I
What: Living preference
When: In the future
Where: Countryside
Why: For a different lifestyle
How: By choosing to relocate

Answer: While the city's allure is undeniable, the countryside's serene and simplistic charm occasionally pulls at my heartstrings, painting a picture of a life unburdened by the relentless urban hustle.

7. What is public transport like in your area?

5W1H Ideas:
Who: I
What: Describing public transport
When: Currently
Where: In my area
Why: To convey the transportation situation
How: Based on personal experience

Answer: The public transport in my area is a double-edged sword; while it's efficient and ubiquitous, it's often crowded, especially during the rush hours, making the commute a test of patience and endurance.

8. Do you have friends or relatives in rural areas?

5W1H Ideas:
Who: I
What: Having acquaintances in rural areas
When: Currently
Where: In rural areas
Why: Due to family or friend connections
How: Maintaining relationships

Answer: Yes, I have relatives tilling the soil in rural landscapes. Visiting them is like turning over a new leaf, with each trip providing a refreshing break from my routine, immersing me in a world where life flows at its own sweet pace.

WEATHER AND SEASONS

1. What's the weather like today in your city?

5W1H Ideas:
Who: The city's residents
What: Experiencing today's weather
When: Today
Where: In my city
Why: Daily weather variation
How: Observationally

Answer: Today, the sun is playing hide and seek behind the clouds in my city, providing us with intermittent warmth. It's a mild day, with a gentle breeze whispering through the trees, creating a pleasant atmosphere.

2. Do you prefer hot or cold weather?

5W1H Ideas:
Who: I
What: Have a weather preference
When: Generally
Where: In any location
Why: Personal comfort and liking
How: By feeling comfortable in specific weather

Answer: I have a penchant for cold weather. There's something inherently cozy and inviting about wearing layers, sipping on hot drinks, and watching the breath fog up in the chilly air.

3. Which season do you enjoy the most?

5W1H Ideas:
Who: I
What: Enjoying a specific season
When: Annually
Where: In my location
Why: Due to personal enjoyment and comfort
How: Engaging in seasonal activities

Answer: Autumn is my cup of tea, with its tapestry of colors painting the landscape, the crisp air signaling a change, and the anticipation of holidays adding a festive cheer to the ambiance.

4. How does the weather affect your mood?

5W1H Ideas:
Who: I
What: Mood affected
When: On different weathers
Where: Generally
Why: Weather's impact on mental state
How: Psychologically

Answer: The weather subtly yet profoundly sways my mood. On bright, sunny days, my spirits are lifted, mirroring the vibrancy outdoors. Conversely, continuous gloomy, rainy days can cast a shadow over my mood, making me feel a bit blue.

5. How do you protect yourself from extreme weather?

5W1H Ideas:
Who: I
What: Protecting myself
When: During extreme weather
Where: Wherever I am
Why: For health and safety
How: By taking precautions

Answer: In scorching summers, I am armed with sunscreen and sunglasses, while in the bone-chilling winters, layers of warm clothing are my shield. Regardless of the season, I adjust my gear and activities to the weather's whims, ensuring both comfort and protection are steadfastly maintained.

6. Does the weather influence your daily plans?

5W1H Ideas:
Who: I
What: Daily plans possibly affected
When: Depending on the weather
Where: In my daily life
Why: Weather impacts the feasibility of plans
How: By causing changes or adjustments to plans

Answer: Indeed, weather plays a pivotal role in orchestrating my daily symphony of activities. A rainy forecast might pour water on my parade of outdoor plans, necessitating a shift towards indoor engagements, while a sunny disposition of the sky sets the stage for ventures under the open heavens.

7. Is there a type of weather you haven't experienced but would like to?

5W1H Ideas:
Who: I
What: Desiring to experience a type of weather
When: In the future
Where: In a different location
Why: For a new experience
How: By traveling or living in a different climate

Answer: I've yet to bear witness to the Northern Lights in a frosty Arctic sky, a spectacle that has long been on my bucket list. The desire to experience this magnetic dance of nature compels me to someday venture into territories where the nights are painted with these iridescent strokes.

8. How does weather affect your choice of clothing?

5W1H Ideas:
Who: I
What: Choice of clothing affected
When: Daily
Where: In my daily life
Why: To stay comfortable and protected
How: By dressing appropriately for the weather

Answer: My wardrobe dances to the tunes of the weather, with airy, light clothing taking center stage in summer, while winters see a lineup of cozy, warm attire. The day's forecast is the invisible stylist dictating my sartorial choices, ensuring I step out not just in style but in comfort.

WORK AND STUDIES

1. What do you do for a living?

5W1H Ideas:
Who: I
What: Working
When: Currently
Where: At my workplace
Why: For income and career
How: Professionally and diligently

Answer: I'm currently navigating through the dynamic landscape of marketing, where creativity and strategy shake hands daily. With a focus on digital platforms, I craft narratives and campaigns that echo the voice of various brands, cultivating engagement and building connections.

2. What do you like most about your studies or work?

5W1H Ideas:
Who: I
What: Enjoying aspects of work or studies
When: Throughout my career or study period
Where: At work or educational institution
Why: Due to personal interest and satisfaction
How: Engaging in enjoyable tasks

Answer: My work's tapestry is woven with threads of creativity and challenge, providing a canvas where each day paints a different picture. The exhilarating rush of brainstorming sessions and the satisfaction of seeing a campaign flourish are the treasures of my professional journey.

3. Do you prefer studying in the morning or at night?

5W1H Ideas:
Who: I
What: Having a preference for study time
When: Either morning or night
Where: At my preferred study space
Why: For better concentration and productivity
How: Based on my daily schedule and energy levels

Answer: The tranquil embrace of the morning, where the world is still shaking off its slumber, offers the ideal ambiance for my studies. With a mind refreshed from night's rest and a day yet untouched by chaos, the dawn's early light provides clarity and focus, essential for absorbing knowledge.

4. How do you manage stress from work or studies?

5W1H Ideas:
Who: I
What: Managing stress
When: When stressed
Where: At home or other relaxing places
Why: To maintain mental health
How: Through various stress-relief techniques

Answer: Crafting a symphony of relaxation, I intertwine moments of meditation, exercise, and hobbies into the fabric of my daily life. These elements form a sanctuary, a haven from the relentless waves of work stress, allowing me to recharge and emerge resilient.

5. Do you often work or study late at night?

5W1H Ideas:
Who: I
What: Working or studying late at night
When: Occasionally
Where: At home or workplace
Why: Due to workload or exam preparation
How: Diligently and with focus

Answer: Occasionally, the mantle of night becomes my silent partner in work or studies. With its tranquil environment, it provides a canvas where productivity paints its strokes uninterrupted, allowing me to delve deeper into tasks at hand.

6. What challenges do you face at work or in studies?

5W1H Ideas:
Who: I
What: Facing challenges
When: During work or study hours
Where: At the workplace or educational institution
Why: Due to job or academic requirements
How: Navigating through various difficulties

Answer: Every day unfurls a new challenge, be it meeting tight deadlines or absorbing complex information. These hurdles, though daunting, are the stepping stones to personal and professional growth, sculpting me into a resilient and adept individual.

7. Do you have a good work-study balance?

5W1H Ideas:
Who: I
What: Maintaining work-study balance
When: Presently
Where: In daily life
Why: For a healthy and balanced lifestyle
How: Through effective time management

Answer: In the grand theatre of life, balancing work and studies is akin to walking a tightrope. Through meticulous planning and a judicious use of time, I've been able to carve out a harmony, allotting adequate time to both realms without compromising on relaxation and personal time.

8. How do you usually get ready for exams or important assignments?

5W1H Ideas:
Who: I
What: Preparing for exams or assignments
When: During exam season or assignment due dates
Where: At home or library
Why: To perform well
How: Through structured preparation and review

Answer: As deadlines or exams loom, I adopt a regimented approach to preparation. Prioritizing topics, creating a schedule, and allowing time for review and relaxation are the bricks building my fortress of readiness, equipping me to face academic challenges head-on.